RICHMOND
INDEPENDENT PRESS

Mary —
Best Wishes!

RICHMOND
INDEPENDENT PRESS

A HISTORY OF THE
UNDERGROUND ZINE SCENE

DALE M. BRUMFIELD

Foreword by Don Harrison; Introduction by Edwin Slipek Jr.

Charleston · London

THE
History
PRESS

Published by The History Press
Charleston, SC 29403
www.historypress.net

Copyright © 2013 by Dale M. Brumfield
All rights reserved

Back cover banana illustration by Mike Cody for the *Richmond Mercury*, 1975. *Courtesy VCU Cabell Library Special Collections, Richmond, Virginnia.*

First published 2013

Manufactured in the United States

ISBN 978.1.60949.839.9

Library of Congress CIP data applied for.

CONTENTS

FOREWORD

It just sounds wrong. A history of the underground press in Richmond, Virginia—the home of Confederate statues, big tobacco, Massive Resistance and Representative Eric Cantor? You might as well publish a book about the history of rhythm and blues in Provo, Utah.

Now, for all I know, Provo's after-hours ski lodge blues dens were that community's shared secret. I anxiously await that book, just as I eagerly anticipated this survey of early underground publishing in Richmond that introduces the world to seminal River City publications such as the *Richmond Afro-American*, *The Ghost*, *The Sunflower* and the *Richmond Chronicle*, among many others.

But *Richmond Independent Press: A History of the Underground Zine Scene* is not only an overview of the dissent, social anxiety and racial divisions found in a midsized southern American city during one of the nation's most turbulent periods, it's also an alternative history of that city as seen from its restless (and still festering) underground—the students, the poets, the artists and the disenfranchised. It's a tale largely never told. And Dale Brumfield is just the right guy to tell it because he was there, as one of the prime movers and shakers in the "Richmond scene."

This city has a thriving "Do it yourself" media landscape these days, with independent radio stations, blogs, 'zines and social media getting the message out. *Richmond Independent Press* is a reminder that this didn't just happen yesterday or in a vacuum. The book also shows us that illuminating history isn't just found in the revelations of new trivia about "Great Men" or pivotal events we already know about; it's also found when assumptions about places and people are challenged and put under the microscope of deep research.

As Brumfield illustrates, Richmond, Virginia, has a long and intricate history of self-published and alternative media, created by individuals trying to make sense of life in a deeply flawed place that they can't help loving anyway. The story is populated with names you may know (Tom Robbins, Frank Rich and Matt Groening), but mainly you will hear from people not so well known, such as John Mitchell, Edward H. Peeples and Bruce Smith—key figures who struggled valiantly to bring to their audiences a perspective markedly different from the one peddled by the area's conservative news dailies, the *Richmond News-Leader* and the *Richmond Times Dispatch*.

So yes, we may be waiting a long time to read about that Mormon blues scene; the architectural photo book of Lost Springs, Wyoming; or the history of surfing in Taos, New Mexico. But we do have this engaging piece of history that tells of the early days of the underground press in Richmond, Virginia, and it's anything but wrong. It turns out to be a great yarn that was just waiting to be retold.

–Don Harrison, May 30, 2013

Don Harrison is a journalist, editor, music archivist, disc jockey and former publisher of Catharsis *(1989–93) and* Grip *(1996–99), Virginia publications deeply inspired by* ThroTTle, *the Richmond tabloid cofounded by Dale Brumfield.*

AUTHOR'S NOTE

These smut sheets are today's Molotov cocktails thrown at respectability and decency in our nation…They encourage depravity and irresponsibility, and they nurture a breakdown in the continued capacity of the government to conduct an orderly and constitutional society.
—Texas congressman and former House Un-American Activities Committee chairman Joe Pool, reported in the Dallas Morning News, *November 7, 1967*

Many historians have eulogized the radical underground '60s "smut sheets" as having failed after enjoying a shelf life of only a few years. The Richmond underground press may have done a lot of things—fallen victim to its own lofty idealism, burned out or went broke—but it did not *fail*. It achieved its purpose of giving a voice to radical criticism and social change, and the legacy passed on by the early "underground" press in the '60s was the "alternative" press that rose up in the '70s and '80s into the '90s before the Internet changed it all. That's not failure. That's innovation, despite what the *Richmond Times Dispatch* may have claimed at the time.

Every effort was made to locate as many independent publications as possible from the 1960–90 era. If one is not here, it is likely that no copies, information or staff members were available, that it fell outside the timeline or, in one case, that no one remembered creating it. I do apologize for any I may have missed. *Style Weekly*—a critical part of Richmond's media landscape—is not here either. It would be unfair to describe thirty-one years of publishing in three thousand words. It needs its own book.

Ladies and gentlemen, boys and girls, it's time to "paste up or shut up."

–DMB

ACKNOWLEDGEMENTS

The author wishes to thank the following people and institutions for their immeasurable and enthusiastic assistance in compiling this history.

Katya Sabaroff Taylor
Dr. Edward H. Peeples
Roy Scherer
Mac McWilliams
Phil Trumbo
Duck Baker
John Harbaugh
Rebby Sharp
Robert Mark
Chuck Wrenn
Deona Landes Houff
Terry Rea
Steve Wall
John Poulos
Blake Slonecker
Bruce Smith
Joe Schenkman
Peter Blake
Rob Sauder-Conrad
Don Harrison

Michael Kaluta
Stephen Hickman
Bill Nelson
Charles Allen Sugg
Garrett Epps
Glenn Frankel
Gene Ely
Bill Kovarik
Ron Thomas Smith
John Williamson
Greg Harrison
Ned Scott Jr.
Caryl Burtner
Michele Houle
Anne Thomas Soffee
Joe Essid
Doug Dobey
Ann Henderson
Paul Ivey
Phil Ford
Juliet Guimont
Jim Drewry
Tom Campagnoli
David Stover
Mariane Matera
Susan Brumfield
John Whiting
Susan Benshoff
Jim Turney
Brooke Saunders
Carol Sutton
Kelly Alder
John Sarvay
Mark Brown
Eddie Peters
John Kneebone
Michael Clautice
Anne Fleischman
Amy Crehore

Andy Fekete
Bill Creekmur
Bunny Creekmur
Sam Forrest
Greg Geddes
Wes Freed
Devon Kestenbaum
Bill Oliver
Karl Waldbauer
Robert Haddow
Edwin Slipek Jr.
Bill Altice
Richard Bland
Thomas Daniel
Hazel Trice Edney
Nick Schrenk
Jeanne Minnix
Sue Dayton
Lori Ellison
David Powers
and Matt Hahn as the Beaver

Thanks to Hunter Brumfield for photography. Special thanks to the Virginia Commonwealth University James Branch Cabell Library, Special Collections and Archives, Richmond, Virginia. Special thanks also to the University of Virginia Alderman Library and the Small Special Collections, Charlottesville, Virginia.

"What's up? Paste up!" (Ronnie Sampson, 1980).

INTRODUCTION

I t's just too easy to live in Richmond. It's a town that has always had the toughest questions to ask, but it's never chosen to ask them. Our native conservatism is a culture fed by southside Virginia. Richmonders for the past seventy-five years are made up of folks who come from an arc that starts in Lynchburg and swings into northern North Carolina and over to Suffolk. In North Carolina, you learn the three Rs: readin', ritin' and the road to Richmond. That's our feeder system—wonderful folks with family and church and good basic rural values who make up what Richmond is. Our young people move on to the next bigger market, D.C. or New York,

Left to right: Richmond artists Charles Vess, Phil Trumbo and Michael Kaluta "faery gazing" in Richmond, Virginia, 1975. *Courtesy Phil Trumbo.*

so we just don't have an aggressive intelligentsia here; we are just a pleasant place with a lot of pleasant people, but nobody has any inkling of how to rock the boat. So it's always fallen to a few people who have always stayed in it, and they've done it since they were teenagers and will do it until they die. That's all you need to know about Richmond.

—Edwin Slipek Jr., April 2, 2013
Former alternative publisher and current *Style Weekly*
senior contributing editor

THE GHOST, 1960–1961

The Fan District, which we are now passing, is Richmond's answer to Greenwich Village in New York.
—overheard spiel aboard a Richmond tourist bus, circa 1959, when passing through the Fan, as reported in The Ghost

While many books over the years have documented the spirits that haunt Richmond, one ghost that appeared on the city streets in 1960 during Richmond's "Beat" period and in the heat of the escalating civil rights era was more interested in alerting people throughout the Fan District and Richmond Professional Institute (RPI) community to such divisive social issues as segregation, racism, police brutality and the unfair treatment of women.

Written in anonymous third person and calling itself the "Verbal consciousness of the Fan District and RPI," *The Ghost* was Richmond's first modern-era dissident publication.

The Ghost had much in common with similar mimeographed publications of the '50s in other cities that emerged from a culture whose writers embraced a more literary standard in their writing and appealed to a much smaller audience. Some historians regard these "little magazines" as an indirect link to the '60s underground press, but the more commonly known "underground" papers that appeared later in the decade were by contrast antagonistically political and more populist and questioned all authority, often even disparaging the authority of commonly accepted literary and journalistic standards.

THE **Ghost**

NEWS and CONTROVERSY

VOL. I NO 1 - Published when Needed - Price: FREE

EDITORIAL

For the past several years, RPI has been the intellectual uterus for hundreds of gifted artists, writers, actors, musicians, and professional people. Through its unique approach to education, it has provided the impetus to talents and capacities far beyond that of any other Virginia school.

Somehow, even in its financial smallness and its physical limits, it has delivered products of creation which have surpassed, magnificently, the button-down degrees, issued at our state's "norm" factories.

RPI's name is reported by the Library of Congress to have one of the 10 finest art schools in America. It is recognized by many outside the state as Virginia's only hope to climb out of the pit of provincialism. Her graduates and certificate bearers distribute their goods throughout the world and the reputation is good because her products have proven it to be good.

RPI, although said by many Virginians, and particularly Richmonders, to be a bedlam of Communists, leftists, beats, and misguided young hoodlems, has gained a level of respect denied it by her very own neighbors. The labels and names born out of ignorance and limit are but a small price to pay for the wonderful things that have been born at this school.

The sour-grapes reaction thrust at students, faculty, and administration, by Fan residents, people of Richmond, and the pressures and fears brought to bear on the administration and thus, on the students, are absolutely unwarranted and have no place in a democracy.

The financial squeeze from the State Legislature and W&M have seemingly started a change of events which is, apparently an all out drive for "lets all be normal" at RPI. We must manufacture "Alvin Average" because it is financially secure; because it is fiscally fit; and because it is All-American.

(Continued on next page.)

INTRODUCTORY WORDS

We feel that the quickest way to introduce The Ghost to our new readers, is to let them read it. We would like you to agree with our views, however disagreement can be healthy.....so long as you do not remain inert.

We feel that the Ghost should be provocative and "newsy" and that it will become the overt voice of your wishes and desires of RPI and the Fan district.

BUCK PASSING

The class in "The Introduction to the Arts" required a group of art and experimental films as part of the class program. The Audio-Visual Aids office turned down the instructor's request for the films because the school could not afford to give $120.00 from its limited budget to a single class.

The instructor informed the class of this, and the class of 75 students pitched in enough money to purchase the films. The Audio-Visual Aids office graciously declined the contributions and provided the films (with much embarrassment.)

The Ghost, volume 1, number 1. *Courtesy VCU Cabell Library Special Collections, Richmond, Virginia.*

Dissident (or pre-underground) publications were unheard of in Richmond during the Eisenhower years and indeed were rarities even throughout the entire nation. In 1958, Paul Krassner founded *The Realist*—a proto-hippie mix of irreverence that focused almost exclusively on satire—which many consider the true father of the underground press. "The *Realist*," commented the *New York Times*, "is the *Village Voice* with its fly open."

At the time of the first edition of *The Ghost*, Richmond (and Virginia) was not just snapping its fingers to Greenwich Village–style Beatnik values but reeling from numerous groundbreaking civil rights events. The Virginia-based 1960 Supreme Court case *Boynton v. Virginia* banned seat segregation on interstate bus service following an incident in Richmond's former Trailways terminal on West Broad Street when a black passenger refused to move from the whites-only section of the terminal restaurant. A year later, the Freedom Riders pulled into Richmond thinking that the bus terminal was segregated but left when they learned it still was not.

Southern Virginia's Prince Edward County Public Schools defiantly closed rather than integrate from 1959 to 1964, causing most of the county's black students to lose most if not all of those years of education. "The County board of supervisors adopted a resolution declaring it will not levy any taxes for public school operations for the fiscal year beginning July 1," noted the page 1 headline in the June 3, 1959 *Richmond Times Dispatch*.

Then, on February 20 and 22, 1960, thirty-four black Virginia Union University students defied segregation downtown by taking seats at the whites-only first-floor lunch counter at the Richmond Room at Thalhimers department store on West Broad Street. While the first sit-in was peaceful, arrests and trumped-up trespassing and conspiracy charges still later failed to deter the protestors, and by August 1961—after an entire year of picketing and boycotts—seven stores, including Thalhimers and Woolworth's, had finally desegregated their lunch counters.

Nine issues of *The Ghost* were "published when needed" and given away for free during this transformative time by Richmond native, Richmond Professional Institute graduate and self-described "twentieth-century scalawag" Edward H. Peeples and his friend, transplanted New Yorker Richard Kollin. Its simple "little magazine" two-column layout (one mimeographed legal-size sheet, typed and printed front and back) belied its mortal wounding of sacred Richmond cows, pulling no punches against the hypocrisy of segregation, brutal police tactics, the unfair treatment of female RPI students by "rude and tactless" dorm mothers and the College of William & Mary's alleged stranglehold on the RPI administration.

"We feel that *The Ghost* should be provocative and 'newsy' and that it will become the overt voice of your wishes and desires of RPI and the Fan District," read the introduction in the first issue. "We would like you to agree with our views; however disagreement can be healthy...so long as you do not remain inert."

Peeples was no stranger to controversy. A 1957 graduate of Richmond Professional Institute and captain of its first winning basketball team, this self-professed "spy for the Black community" (despite his white ancestry) was active in civil rights movements as a student and then participated in the downtown sit-ins protesting segregation with other Richmond notables such as Edward Meeks Gregory and L. Douglas Wilder, who went on to become the United States' first black governor from 1990 to 1994. "I was never arrested, not once," Peeples insisted in a 2011 interview, "but I have been thrown out and fired from a whole lot of places."

After a post-graduation stint in the navy, Peeples returned to Richmond in 1959. "I was excited to be back and connecting with the Richmond radicals— both of them," he said. He went to work in the welfare department, where he witnessed a startling amount of workplace segregation, telling Kent Willis in a 1984 interview in the *Raleigh Review*, "Black caseworkers were on one side of the office and whites on the other." He also started hanging around the 800 and 900 blocks of West Grace Street, where that year (as reported in issue 4 of *The Ghost*), 85 percent of all Richmond's felony arrests occurred.

"The Village Restaurant was the gathering place," Peeples said of the restaurant at its former location on the southeast corner of Grace and Harrison Streets, explaining that all the special interests—including the communists, the leftists, the beats and the artists—blocked out their own little corners to pontificate on their pet causes. He added that there was also at that time a subculture of "button-down" *Richmond News-Leader* opinion editor James J. Kilpatrick "wannabes" who espoused white supremacy. "They stood around in their handsome attire and loafers and talked among themselves."

"Of course, there are a multitude of phonies," noted issue 4 of *The Ghost*. "There are the giddy and the verbose who scream at the top of their voices 'I am an artist!' 7 nights a week. The counterfeit poets, always ready to stick their latest ineffectiveness under your nose. And then the inevitable prostitutes, teenage hoods, winos and panhandlers."

"Richmond truly had a strong Beat community in the '50s, very much so," said retired Fan District resident Bill Creekmur. "There also was a strong intellectual gay community that contributed to this whole scene, and the Village was a strong melting pot for this."

"A Beatnik led a different life than the academic poet," wrote art historian, author and former Fan District resident Robert Haddow in a 2012 correspondence. "We lived in flophouses and slept by the side of the road. We did a million different things but never the careful, cultivated career thing. We knew who each other were like ex-cons recognize one another. We were scarred, screwed-up scrappers."

Not just the Village but also Richmond's entire Fan District became a major player in the birth of the counterculture during this critical late 1950s to early 1960s period. Ed Steinberg's Meadow Laundry across Harrison Street (where the Village Restaurant is located today) displayed local artwork for the students, panhandlers and Beatniks to enjoy while they did their washing and folding, earning a gracious mention in *The Ghost*: "The Meadow Laundry, we feel, is one of the cultural bright spots in the fan district, and consequently, deserves the complete support of RPI students and Fan residents…Besides all this, they do a good machine load of rough-dry."

Up the block, the Lee Theater—after being closed for three years—reopened on Christmas Day 1959 as an alternative/foreign film venue earning a bravo: "*The Ghost* offers three hearty cheers to the Lee Theater opening…and particularly for [the Ingmar Bergman film] 'Wild Strawberries.' We need the Lee Theater, and they need us. Support them."

A few doors down and across the street from the Lee Theater, Sanford Ruben opened Sandor's Book Store (named for him and his wife, Doris), and also on this strip was the presence of a reputed gay beer joint, called Eton's Inn. Eton's was opened originally in about 1947 by the Rotella brothers, one of whom was head of the local musicians union and later did bookings for the former Mosque (now the Altria Theater). By 1960, Eton's, like the Village, had become a hangout for Richmond's artistic, gay and avant-garde communities.

"Back then, Eton's was divided in thirds, with no walls," said Bill Creekmur. "The first third was heterosexual, the second third was gay guys and the final third would be lesbians."

"Eton's had a large circular table at the front that seated some of Richmond's early avant-garde such as Bill Jones, Susan Bush, Ray Herman, Chuck Diamond, Paul Miller, Faith Butler, Gypsy, Lester Blackiston, Kenny Potts et al.," wrote artist Eddie Peters. "Norman Lassiter eventually moved to NYC where he ran a silk screen operation and did many screens for Andy Warhol. Tom Robbins was also an early character and was close friends with Bill Jones as well as Bill Kendrick. Pat Williams was part of this early bohemian scene and purportedly was a model for a character in Robbins' book *Even Cowgirls Get the Blues*."

One of Richmond's more unique (and some say obnoxious) poetic talents, Lester Blackiston was at the epicenter of artistic literary activity in the late 1950s. Blackiston would go to the Village Restaurant or Eton's Inn and then walk down the aisles, loudly reading poetry and demanding to know if his work was worth money. Friends claimed that people sometimes paid the volatile poet to just make him leave. He was rumored to have thrown a dead cow into the Shockoe Bottom locks to force the city to pump it out and stolen an original Modigliani painting from the Phillips Gallery in Washington, D.C., discretely returning it when publicity got too intense.

A vitriolic presence who frequently spewed angry tirades, Blackiston was friends with both Norman Mailer (author and cofounder of the *Village Voice* in 1954) and the notoriously secretive Ezra Pound. Blackiston even used to visit Pound at St. Elizabeth's Mental Hospital in the 1950s when Pound was held there while accused of treason. He frequently picked fights during his outbursts, and more than once, he reportedly pulled a gun or a switchblade, supposedly not to actually cut but just to flash the tip in someone's face.

"Lester was a piece of work," said Bill Creekmur. "I saw him take a pistol out of a Bible where he had it cut out and shoot at a guy at a party one night." Bunny Creekmur added that she also saw Lester take out a gun and shoot it through the roof of his houseboat, on which he lived in Richmond's Shockoe Bottom.

"I found Lester to be…unpleasant," said Richmond native Roy Scherer, choosing his words. "I thought he treated his wife, Lilly, like shit. I was not friends; I was acquainted. He was not my friend."

"I saw Lester as an asshole," wrote former Fan resident Susan Benshoff in 2012. "When we were on 18th Street Lester would get drunk and come pee in the alley and rant—or spout poetry, there was a fine line here. We all thought he was a pain in the ass, including the old lady that lived over 'Bird in Hand' that would dump buckets of water on him."

"Lester lived longer because he was stronger," wrote Robert Haddow. "No career. No pension. No tenure. No wonder he was crazy. A real Beatnik. But less of a poet. Much less."

Another Beatnik poet, James Patrick "Rik" Davis, also first showed up in town in about 1958, fresh from poetry gigs at the Lighthouse Club in Hermosa Beach, California, where as an eighteen-year-old he recited on the same stage as Allen Ginsburg and Philip Whalen. In Richmond, he fell in with Blackiston and the Grace Street crowd (and especially with young women) at the Village Restaurant, writing poetry out of love and later pornography out of financial necessity.

"Rik read *On the Road* and took off, hoping that he would meet the other beats in bars and flophouses on the West Coast and Manhattan," wrote Haddow. "Rik and I hit it off because we'd both clocked thousands of miles the hard way. All that in the service of literature and poetry."

"Rik, I liked and admired," said Scherer. "He was the unacknowledged VIP in the subculture around the fan."

Author Tom Robbins at this time wrote columns for the *Proscript*, the RPI school newspaper, entitled "Robbins Nest" and "Walks on the Wild Side" that frequently described his experiences at Eton's and West Grace Street. "West Grace Street takes on an insect quality in the spring," he wrote. "People swarm over the front porches and over the front steps of every 'Beat' apartment house."

"A town's true personality is reflected not in its main streets, but in its alleys," he continued. "I've toured the narrow arteries and cowpaths of more than a few American cities, but in none was there anything approaching the lush, delicate beauty of the Fan District alleys in springtime."

Although he was fearless in fighting racial and sexual inequities in the mid-1950s as an RPI student, Peeples and cofounder Dick Kollin less than three years later chose to publish *The Ghost* anonymously. Kollin was still active duty at the time as an army intelligence officer, and his exposure in the publication may have jeopardized his military status.

"Your part in maintaining *The Ghost* is NOT spreading rumors about the identity of the editors!" warned a blurb on the front of volume 1, number 2.

The Ghost was born out of Peeples's frustration not just with RPI's relationship with Richmond but also with a euphemistic approach toward segregation coined by *Richmond News-Leader* editor Douglas Southall Freeman as "the Virginia Way." White Virginia considered itself a refined exception to the more blatantly exploitive racial systems of the Deep South, and "the Virginia Way" afforded Virginia that latitude to "segregate like a gentleman," not like those "rubes in Alabama who give segregation a bad name."

"Kilpatrick is the one who in my opinion created the entire resistance movement throughout the south," Peeples said in the 1984 Willis interview. "He and William Simmons of the White Citizens Council in Mississippi were bosom buddies in the '50s. Together, they developed an elaborate Massive Resistance ideology."

Peeples explained that part of the Virginia Way was to respond with silence to Richmond's tacit acceptance of that southern intolerance and of hesitation to embrace the sweeping tide of integration. "But there were many people too who supported what we did but also did not speak out."

NEWS and CONTROVERSY

VOL I NO 2 - Published When Needed - Price : FREE

EDITORIAL

It was recently observed by The Ghost that a basketball game between RPI and Union Theological Seminary scheduled for January 5 was mysteriously called off. It seems that there is a negro player on Union's team, and there is a vague policy, enforced by some equally vague bureaucrat, somewhere in the W&M administrative scheme, restricting RPI and Norfolk Division from competing in athletics against anyone but bright blue-eyed Aryans.

It is said that it is fine and dandy and brotherly lovely to play ball against negroes, so long as you don't play on state property. (You all know the tradition.)

Now, as to where the decree came from, The Ghost can only afford to speculate, but all information gives the impression that the Board of Visitors in Williamsburg has its strong hands firmly around the neck of RPI officials. Whether or not the RPI administration has surrendered all autonomy is still in question. No matter who the individuals or group who have imposed this policy of all white sports competition, The Ghost would like the RPI and Fan public to be aware of the fact that THERE IS NO STATE LAW RESTRICTING WHITES AND NEGROES FROM COMPETING IN ATHLETICS.

The Ghost has searched extensively the State Constitution, the Codes of Virginia, and the Acts of the Assembly, Special Session, 1959, and found nothing in these documents relating to white-negro athletic competition nor the use of state property for such competition. We also questioned officials of the General Assembly and they knew nothing of such laws.

Now if RPI is a state school and is so devoted to the strict obeyence of the state law, why would they employ such a smear-inviting policy. There are elements in the race conflict who would delight in making a neon-bright issue of this incident. Also Union Theological Seminary is quite upset.

We ask our readers what this incident means in terms of RPI's

(Continued on next page)

SOME ADDITIONAL WORDS

The Ghost, of course, has ears and has heard criticisms and favorable remarks concerning our first issue. We are quite pleased with both responses and hope that we can continue to be the verbal conscience of the Fan district and RPI, and even to bring about some desirable changes in our community and school. Not believing in purposeless, destructive criticism, we hope that our censure of current practices employed by the state, city, and RPI officials can provoke only good. We simply wish to impress upon these public servants that the democratic process demands that institutions and officials maintain a flexible character and a sensitive responsiveness to constructive change.

YOUR PART IN MAINTAINING THE GHOST IS NOT SPREADING RUMORS ABOUT THE IDENTITY OF THE EDITORS!

TO RUDE AND TACTLESS DORM MOTHERS

(And not all of them are.).

The Ghost does hereby and herein proclaim that students, from this time onward, are to be considered in the classification of Homo Sapien and be afforded all the rights, and priviledges, and immunities normaly included therein.

The Ghost, volume 1, number 2. *Courtesy VCU Cabell Library Special Collections, Richmond, Virginia.*

Peeples explained that his awareness of the Virginia Way and the attitude of William & Mary toward RPI at that time clarifies the political and cultural environment in which *The Ghost* was launched. "RPI got nothing from William & Mary," he explained, and apparently very little from Richmond too. RPI was considered a blue-collar school—"College for the rest of us" according to him and "a hotbed of slanderous stereotypes" according to the local media.

"RPI, although said by many Virginians, and particularly Richmonders, to be a bedlam of communists, leftists, beats, and misguided young hoodlums, has gained a level of respect denied it by her very own neighbors," noted the lead editorial in issue number 1. "The labels and names born out of ignorance and limit are but a small price to pay for the wonderful things that have been born at this school."

The Virginia Way also did not stress college education, Peeples said, claiming that Virginia at that time had the second-lowest number of college-age young people enrolled in college, just above Mississippi. "The saying then was 'thank God for Mississippi.'"

Despite being cast as "communists, leftists and misguided young hoodlums," the RPI students still maintained an ass-kicking attitude, and a handful of faculty members—including Alice Davis, Raymond Hodges, Theresa Pollak and Dr. Henry Hibbs—were instrumental in keeping the fiercely dedicated young students pointed in productive directions.

"[Dr.] Hibbs got nothing from William & Mary, yet he managed to buy up a lot of property [for the school], and I'm sure he did some of it illegally," Peeples claimed, reminding that the campus did not get a new building until the Franklin Street Gym was built in 1952.

"That was the first building of any kind that was built from the ground up from 1917 to 1951," said Virginius Dabney (who served as rector of the Virginia Commonwealth University Board of Visitors in 1968 and 1969) in a 1985 *Commonwealth Times* interview. "Even the head of the English department had to teach in basements, attics and furnace rooms until he finally got a little room over on Floyd Avenue."

Despite RPI's reputation as a rough-and-tumble southern working-class upstart, it attracted a large number of northerners, mostly due to the enormous respect that Art School founder Theresa Pollak commanded in New York. The RPI art enclave's creeping bohemianism must also have become a threat not only to the traditional liberal arts mentality but also to the city at large. "The question must be answered," *The Ghost* asked, "will RPI continue to grow into an intellectual and creative workshop or will it assume striped-tic-and-branch-water academics?"

Even in 1968, when RPI finally became Virginia Commonwealth University (VCU), the school maintained an avant-garde, somewhat radical image and was referred to by many old Richmond residents as "Viet Cong University."

In addition to expounding on the inequities of the RPI–William & Mary arrangement and the racist and anti-college "Virginia Way," *The Ghost* also exposed racial inequities in college sports. An editorial in number 2 described how a basketball game between RPI and Union Theological Seminary scheduled a month before the downtown sit-ins on January 5, 1960, was "mysteriously called off": "It seems there is a negro player on Union's team, and there is a vague policy, enforced by some equally vague bureaucrat somewhere in the W&M administrative scheme, restricting RPI and Norfolk Division from competing in Athletics against anyone but bright blue-eyed Aryans."

After pointing out that there was no state law restricting whites and blacks from competing in athletics, *The Ghost* noted that "in the past, negroes have played on the RPI gym floor…No defamation resulted and most important, there were no black footprints embedded in the gym floor after the game!"

Suffocating student regulations under the presidency of Dr. George Oliver and, especially, housing rules imposed on female RPI students by "dorm mothers" were frequent hot topics in *The Ghost*: "Here at RPI, in the second half of the twentieth century, we still enjoy the puritanical delusion that a thick, gooey subterfuge of archaic rules will preserve the chastity and repute" of the females. Another short in number 3, entitled "WACS," pointed out that single women who served in the United States Army were perceived as a possible threat to the innocence of the younger females and not permitted to live in RPI dorms. "It seems the administration feels these girls are much too worldly for OUR little women!"

A regular column in the first several issues titled "Les Gendarmes" chronicled the heavy-handed Richmond police presence. A cartoon on the front of number 3 shows a snarling police dog on a leash with the caption, "The Ghost humbly submits this drawing to the city council as a possible substitution for the present Richmond city seal," echoing a famous 1960 photograph appearing in the *Times Dispatch* that drew unwanted national attention to Ruth Tinsley—the wife of the then state National Association for the Advancement of Colored People (NAACP) president Dr. J.M. Tinsley—being manhandled across Broad Street by two city policemen and a police dog.

The Ghost

NEWS AND CONTROVERSY!!

VOL.I NO.4 - PUBLISHED WHEN NEEDED - PRICE: FREE

END OF THE YEAR

One of The Ghost's assistant editors suggested, the other day, that as long as this issue would be the last Ghost of the school year, (we're not sure about a Summer Ghost) we should put out a "family-size" issue which would be something of a no-holds-barred issue.

After cold compresses were applied, and after a few dozen wrist-slaps, the editor regained consciousness, mumbling something about the state penitentiary and compromising with the powers that be and after a magnificent inter-nacine battle, this issue is what resulted.

EDITORIAL

The City of Richmond and the State of Virginia are currently preparing their arsenals for a stupendous reproduction of one of the most internationally embarrassing and certainly the saddest page in our history: the Civil War.

Now, after nearly 100 years, we practical and frugal Virginians, lead by the twisted economical precepts of the honorable king of the congressional budget cutters, Harry Byrd Sr., are to embark on a giddy, inane voyage to the world of of lets pretend. It seems we are going to have a multi-million dollar Civil War celebration to honor the time when our democratic state fondled slavery. It seems that we are going to celebrate blood and war. We are, with the supposedly economical Mr. Byrd lookin on, going to squander public money into a compulsive southern fixation which we would like to term nectal-spect.

It would not be so bad for us to spend our own public money for an ugly skeleton occasionally, but it keeps us uneasy when we see that within the past 5 years or so, we have spent countless millions from the state treasury on such items as a functionless war memorial on Belvedere Street to say nothing of the multi-million dollar Jamestown festival, to name a few.

Our schools and mental institutions are ranked frighteningly low (Continued on next page)

GRACE STREET

If the RPI Administration, faculty, and students, along with Fan merchants, and residents would complain long and loudly enough to City Hall about the slum conditions in the 800 and 900 blocks of Grace Street, the city could effect considerable change and improvemnt in this area. The Ghost has learned from reliable sources that almost 85% of arrests in 1959, in the Fan, were for felonies committed by residents "and their guests" of these two blocks.

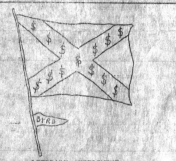

LITERARY SUPPLEMENT

The editors of The Ghost could not come anywhere near approaching agreement on what should be said concerning the Proscript Literary Supplement. Opinions varied from near euphoria to almost total disgust. So in order to avoid the added expense of body guards etc., we're begging out and not making any comments on it in this issue.

ONE DAY FOR EACH FOOT

"After all" she thought, "I'm here to study so it doesn't matter where." But is did matter! She was 10 feet in front of the reception desk from 10 PM to 11 PM. Result – 10 days strict campus and an awareness that studying isn't always the big thing at RPI.

The Ghost, volume 1, number 4. *Courtesy VCU Cabell Library Special Collections, Richmond, Virginia.*

After several issues, author Tom Robbins contributed a few short columns to *The Ghost*. "Robbins wrote satires but was not interested in the social issues," Peeples explained. "He just enjoyed savaging southern culture."

Despite Robbins's talents as a writer and his affection for Richmond and its people, his promotion of recreational drug use to teenagers eventually drove a wedge between him and Peeples, who was against illicit drug use. Although remaining friends, their partnership dissolved. Robbins went on to work for the *Richmond Times Dispatch* as a sports writer and copy editor before he moved out west to become a best-selling novelist.

Despite all of its reasons for existing, *The Ghost* was never interested in the name-calling and nonobjective advocacy journalism espoused years later by more militant underground publications. "Not believing in purposeless, destructive criticism, we hope that our censure of current practices employed by the state, city and RPI officials can provoke only good," noted issue number 2. "We simply wish to impress upon those public servants that the democratic process demands that institutions and officials maintain a flexible character and a sensitive responsiveness to constructive change."

"We were Shakers, not movers," Peeples said, recalling an Adlai Stevenson rally organized in Monroe Park in 1960 that drew "about a dozen" supporters and four dogs, although Stevenson himself did not show.

In late 1961, *The Ghost* ceased publication when Peeples left Richmond to pursue his graduate degree in human relations at the University of Pennsylvania.

Peeples's concerns for the state of race relations in Virginia prompted him to return to Virginia to research his thesis, "A Perspective of the Prince Edward County School Issue." From 1961 to 1963, he took more than one hundred photographs and interviewed about three hundred people regarding that county's school crisis, including the segregated whites-only private schools established after the public schools closed, illustrating the stark lack of resources the Commonwealth of Virginia and the County of Prince Edward allocated for its black students.

In 2013, Edward H. Peeples remains as fiercely loyal to his alma mater as to the social causes he pursued more than fifty years ago. "You know," he said, "RPI has still been around longer than VCU."

Ghost copublisher Richard Kollin passed away in 2010.

THE MINORITY PRESSES, 1960–1990

The Afro, then at the corner of Third and Clay Streets, was a headquarters for justice in the former capital of the Confederacy. My tenure [there], I believe, remained in sync with the founding purpose of the Black Press in 1827, pleading our own cause, "for too long have others spoken for us."
—Journalist and Howard University professor Hazel Trice Edney in a 2013 correspondence

Τhe reason the paper was founded was that the Black community felt it had no voice," *Richmond Afro-American* editor John Templeton told the Associated Press in 1983. "That basically has not changed over the past 100 years." One hundred years earlier, in 1883, the *Afro-American* was founded as the *Richmond Planet* by Richmond city councilman John Mitchell. The son of slaves, Mitchell championed minority rights when civil rights were nonexistent and lynchings commonplace. In 1892, the *Afro-American* group was founded and began branching into other cities under the leadership of John H. Murphy Sr., his son, George, and his four grandsons—David, Daniel, John and Carl Murphy. Detailed records from the 1920s up into the '30s reveal the skillful financial acumen of the founders, with an accumulation of real estate and equipment almost unheard of by black businesses at the time. In July 1937, the trademark and name "Afro-American" was registered at the U.S. Patent Office.

"A newspaper succeeds because it believes in itself, in God, and in the present generation," stated the "Afro Credo," composed Christmas Day

Richmond Afro-American, April 6, 1968. *Courtesy VCU Cabell Library, Richmond, Virginia.*

1920 by John Murphy Sr. "It must always ask itself if it has kept faith with the common people; whether it has no other goal except to see that liberties are preserved and their future assured; whether it is fighting to get rid of slums, to provide jobs for everybody; whether it stays out of politics except to expose corruption and condemn injustice, race prejudice and the cowardice of compromise."

In 1938, the company purchased the *Richmond Planet* newspaper and changed the name to the *Richmond Afro-American-Planet*, with the first issue printed on June 4, 1938. "Here is our hand, Richmond," stated the announcement of the merger in that first combined issue, written by Editor J. Robert Smith. "We are fully conscious of the responsibility which the assignment as editor of the merges *Planet* and *Afro* imposes, and it shall be our aim to carry on in keeping with the well-established policies of these two journals."

In its heyday, after World War II and into the early 1960s, the *Afro-American* company had thirteen weekly papers in as many cities up and down the East Coast, with a combined circulation of about 225,000. As a young boy, former Virginia governor L. Douglas Wilder delivered the Richmond edition door to door.

The dawning of the civil rights era provoked some of the strongest news coverage and commentary in the *Afro-American*. While the '60s saw many minority groups including blacks, Chicanos, women, gays and others begin their uphill battles for equal rights, Richmond was the epicenter of the black civil rights movement from the late 1950s forward. The state, city and mainstream daily papers' reputation of supporting Massive Resistance had been evident since May 1954, when Chief Justice Earl Warren read the ruling on *Brown v. Board of Education* outlawing segregation in public schools. Virginia senator Harry Byrd declared the ruling "the most serious blow that has yet been struck against the rights of the states." Governor Thomas Stanley said, "I shall use every legal means at my command to continue segregated schools in Virginia."

In 1959, when Prince Edward County voted to close its public schools rather than comply with court-ordered desegregation, affected white students attended segregated private education in churches, lodge halls "and other makeshifts." Over three-quarters of black Prince Edward students, however, lost some or all of those years of education, prompting a visit to Richmond by Dr. Martin Luther King in September 1959. He led a march of more than two thousand people from the Mosque to the state capitol "in a non-violent protest" against the school shutdown.

"We must work for first-class citizenship, but never use second-class methods to gain it," King was quoted in a September 19, 1959 *Afro* article by Ruth Jenkins, which went on to point out that "many colored children are already attending school in adjacent counties while families of others are planning to leave this tobacco-growing county for other parts of the state and nation."

"While a private foundation has been set up to operate a private segregated system for white pupils," the *Afro* noted, "foundation officials claimed that colored community leaders approached them asking about provisions for schooling colored children, [but] told them that they could expect no foundation funds."

The *Afro* reported that up to fifty black students drove daily down to Kittrell Junior College in North Carolina, which had a "high school branch." One man discreetly drove almost twenty black children to an Appomattox school every day. By late September 1959, forty-two of Prince Edward County's seventy black teachers had found jobs in other counties. One teacher, Mrs. Ethel Wilson, applied for a teaching position in Norfolk but was told that they were not accepting applications from "displaced persons."

While the Federal Bureau of Investigation (FBI) would see to it later in the decade that hippies would not be welcome in Richmond, the city saw to it that black entertainers were not as welcome either. A story in the October 1, 1959 *Afro* described a situation when rock-and-roll performer Chuck Berry landed at Byrd Field (now Richmond International Airport) for a concert at the former Richmond Arena on Boulevard after being jailed in Meridian, Mississippi, "on charges of trying to make a date with a white girl at a high school fraternity dance where he was the featured attraction."

After landing in Richmond, Berry spent "an inordinately long time" at the car rental only to be told that despite making a reservation, no rentals were available. A car eventually took him into Richmond, where a rental car was located.

The *Afro* did not always focus solely on racial inequities. "Richmond Social Whirl" by Estelle Clark was a society column much like similar ones in the *Times Dispatch* and *News-Leader*. "This Week's Newsmakers" was a collection of national news service shorts. "Feminine Front" was the women's pages, and there was a similar "Family Front" with articles of interest to parents and families. There was a comics page for the kids.

Then, in 1965, *Afro-American* company publisher Carl Murphy sent a firebrand reporter named Raymond H. Boone to Richmond as editor to boost circulation back to previous 1950s levels. A native of Suffolk, Virginia,

Boone held a bachelor's degree in journalism from Boston University and a master's degree in political science from Howard University. He got his start as a reporter for the *Quincy* (Massachusetts) *Patriot-Ledger* and a sports writer for the *Suffolk News-Herald* in 1956, writing for what were known as the "colored pages" of that newspaper. He was hired to cover the Johnson administration for the *Afro-American* in 1964, and his reputation as a tough, uninhibited reporter caught Murphy's eye and landed him the editorship.

"The circulation was sinking and the paper was gasping for breath," Boone told *Style Weekly*'s Scott Bass in 2011.

"Years before my arrival, *Afro* editor Ray Boone spent decades there, journalistically leading the city through tumultuous racial strife and segregation to its first majority black city council and beyond," said Hazel Trice Edney, who worked as a journalist at the *Afro* from 1987 to September 1991. "Those years were crucial for me as a journalist."

Former *Richmond Mercury* founder and editor Garrett Epps once called Boone the best boss he ever had while working as a reporter for the paper in 1974. Epps recalled in *Style Weekly* that on his first day at the *Afro*, Boone called him in and explained the paper's front-page philosophy: "There are three things that sell newspapers: sex, blood and money," he said. "We try to have all three on every front page."

Epps recalled that Boone could somehow be friends with many of Richmond's most offending segregationist politicians at the time. "The interesting thing to me about Ray, in addition to his absolute commitment to the goals of the Civil Rights movement, he was really good friends with a number of figures you'd think he'd hate," Epps said, including former lieutenant governor Fred Pollard, who ran a racially divisive campaign for that position in 1965.

"[Boone] believed in sound ethics and good journalism," said Douglas C. Lyons in the *Palm Beach Sun-Sentinel*. "Accuracy, brevity and clarity were his ABCs and, boy, did he run a tight ship and expect nothing but your best."

With Boone as editor, and with a hardworking team of reporters led by Detroit native Barry Barkan, the *Afro* was at the forefront of both the civil rights and the New Left movements in Richmond throughout the late 1960s. The divide between the *Afro* and the mainstream Richmond papers—especially the *News-Leader* and its editor, James J. Kilpatrick—was never more apparent than during this period. Kilpatrick's views on race issues came to light after that 1954 *Brown* decision, in which through a series of editorials he justified an old doctrine called interposition, in which individual states had the constitutional duty to introduce their separate sovereignties against federal court rulings that went beyond their rightful powers and, if necessary, strike them down.

The *Afro*, in turn, almost never adopted the ranting anger of Kilpatrick, choosing instead to utilize almost purely objective reporting and to espouse Dr. Martin Luther King's more levelheaded methods of editorial persuasion. "Active resistance on one hand and active love for the opposition on the other are together a powerful harmony," King stated in front of the Mosque, as reported by the *Afro*. Despite the obvious inequities in even the darkest days of the civil rights movement, the *Afro* never resorted to angry, lurid or advocacy journalism like that embraced by many more radical papers in the underground press.

Richmond city councilman Howard Carwile was a friend of the impoverished and frequent contributor to the *Afro* in the late 1960s, delivering his inimitable grasp of the English language to issues pertinent to not just blacks but hippies and the disenfranchised across the city as well. He wrote in the February 5, 1968 issue that "any office holder or candidate for public office whose first allegiance is to the poor and oppressed inevitably finds himself a target for the malicious hate and bigotry of spiteful little pusillanimous panjandrums of loathsome bureaucracy and entrenched oligarchy."

Questionable objectives in a proposed redevelopment of Richmond's heavily black Fulton Bottom brought more strong language from Carwile: "After the [1968] election, these cruel and unscrupulous bureaucrats of diabolical duplicity and loathsome oligarchy will then brazenly come forward with all their brutal plans for annihilating the homes of the poor in Fulton."

The April 4, 1968 assassination of Dr. Martin Luther King dominated the April 13 edition. An article on page 3 was critical of Governor Mills Godwin's rejecting an NAACP invitation to attend a memorial service on the state capitol steps because he claimed he had to "fulfill a long-standing commitment." The *Afro* later learned that he spent the weekend vacationing in Williamsburg.

An above-the-masthead story by Barry Barkan in the May 18, 1968 issue proved again that Richmond's disdainful attitude toward black entertainers had changed little since 1959. Barkan wrote that Richmond's department of parks and recreation, which managed the Mosque, had "slammed the door" on future performances by both James Brown and Jackie Wilson, both of whom had appeared there in the past.

Parks department chief Marshal Rotella said that Brown had been banned "because of the conduct he shows when he appears here," which included jumping from the stage and "hugging and kissing" women in the audience.

Full Coverage Of Dr. King's Life, Death -- 'I Have A Dream' Text

4,000 Virginians Honor Dr. King

Richmond Afro-American

AND THE RICHMOND PLANET

Godwin Vacations While State Mourns

86th Year, No. 27   RICHMOND, VA., APRIL 13, 1968   32 PAGES ★★★ 20 CENTS

'FREE AT LAST'

Housing bill makes progress

150,000 attend Dr. King's rites

Violence, unrest across Nation

Search for killer in Mexico

3 to run for council

City takes 'weak' stand

City a bit cooler now

Richmond Afro-American, April 13, 1968. *Courtesy VCU Cabell Library, Richmond, Virginia.*

"It's likely to cause a problem," Rotella said, adding that he may reconsider if Brown promised to stay onstage while performing.

Jackie Wilson was banned for supposedly having "a bad record of not appearing for engagements," stemming from an incident with a fundraiser at the Sertoma Club January 6 of that year. When a representative of the club was not at the Washington airport to pick him up, Wilson drove himself to Richmond "despite a driving snowstorm." As Wilson arrived at the club, the crowd was leaving.

Rotella said that he decided to ban the two performers because of a "moral obligation" to protect the interests of the people of Richmond. "If something were to go wrong, people would blame the city," he told the *Afro*.

In 1976, after more than a decade editing Richmond's *Afro-American*, Ray Boone was promoted to vice-president and editor of all thirteen editions of the newspapers. He remained at this job for five years but left the company in 1981 due to unspecified "internal problems" with the Murphy family.

The *Afro* hired John W. Templeton, journalism honors graduate from the first freshman class of the Howard University School of Communications, as editor in 1981 to replace Boone and staunch its declining readership, which according to the *1982 Editor & Publisher Yearbook* had dropped from a paid circulation of twenty thousand in the 1940s to about seven thousand. Many minority papers across the United States at that time had experienced serious readership declines as blacks won important civil rights struggles. "Folks figure the struggle was over," Templeton told Associated Press writer Todd Shields in June 1983. "Why read the *Afro*?"

By redrawing the paper's emphasis on state and local news, Templeton brought the *Afro* back to its mid-1970s circulation levels of about twelve thousand. "The *Afro* has given the black community in Richmond and throughout the state a different perspective on what's happening," said James Ghee, then president of the state NAACP. "[It's] a different commentary on the issues than what would be found in the majority newspapers."

In March 1987, the *Afro* hired Louisa, Virginia native Hazel Trice Edney, and she recalled one story that still sticks with her. "It was a sweltering 90-something degrees and the line of Black people stretched at least two blocks along the side street in Downtown Richmond," she wrote in 2013:

> *I'd passed it each month in the bitter cold of winter and the sweltering summer heat. This time, my curiosity got the best of me—it was a line of people waiting for their food stamps. Inside the small distribution center,*

there was no air conditioning in the summer; no water to refresh the people whether elderly, sick or pregnant...A week later, I'd published the story in the Afro. *In response, the Richmond City Manager canceled the contract with the owner of that facility, opening a new center with greater compassion for humanity. Food stamp pick up was changed to a stagger system to end the long lines of all the recipients coming at once. This story was my legacy as a reporter at the* Richmond Afro *Newspaper.*

Edney said that for more than four years, she cut her teeth in journalism at the *Afro*. "[I wrote] stories that impacted public policy and changed conditions on behalf of the truly disadvantaged," she said, "from the food stamp lines to Black contractor participation to police brutality to stories of prison inhumanities."

Despite a cosmetic overhaul and an attempt at free distribution in an effort to win readership and raise revenue in 1993, the *Richmond Afro-American* under publisher John J. Oliver ceased publication on February 13, 1996, ironically in the middle of Black History Month. Citing the increasing cost of newsprint, dropping advertising revenues and competition from former editor Raymond Boone and his paper the *Richmond Free Press*, "the longest running weekly Black newspaper in America," the legacy of Mitchell's *Richmond Planet* finally came to an end in Richmond, leaving only two editions left, in Baltimore and Washington, D.C.

An editorial in the final edition searched for a silver lining to the shutdown: "The decision to close our Richmond publication clears the way for making the Baltimore and Washington operations even stronger with new opportunities to report the news from a Black perspective both locally and nationally."

"The *Afro-American* Newspapers [*sic*] is proud to have 'fought the good fight' here in Richmond," the editorial continued. "We have remained true to our founding mission—we have kept the public faith."

The legacy of the *Afro-American* includes the *Richmond Free Press*. After leaving the *Afro* in 1981, Ray Boone became an associate professor of journalism at Howard University for almost ten years. In 1991, he moved back to Richmond, where he founded Paradigm Communications and started the *Free Press*, with the first issue arriving on newsstands on January 16, 1992. The cover story of that issue analyzed then governor L. Douglas Wilder's withdrawal from the presidential race.

"Richmond, long stagnated in the information and ideas department by a monopolistic daily press, desperately needs a strong gust of fresh air to vigorously fan the expression of ideas about public policy and, in the process, to encourage wide-open, uninhibited debate," read the *Free Press*'s mission on page A4, concluding, "We will do the right thing."

"In 1991, Mr. Boone recruited me as his first reporter for the *Richmond Free Press*, which continued the important journalistic work of breaking racial and economic barriers," wrote Edney. "After more than seven years under what I have come to call his 'Marine boot camp' for journalists, I was awarded a fellowship on the 'press, politics and public policy' at Harvard University, which is the reason I departed Richmond in 1998."

The *Free Press* takes great pride in being part of the Richmond downtown landscape. It was located both at 201 and 101 West Broad Street before moving to its current location at Fifth and Franklin Streets in a building that was originally the American headquarters of the Imperial Tobacco Company of London.

In 2013, Raymond Boone is still editor of the *Free Press*, and Hazel Trice Edney is editor-in-chief of the Trice Edney News Wire and president and CEO of Trice Edney Communications. She was the recipient of the New America Media's (NAM) Ethnic Media "Career Achievement Award" in 2010. She is also proud of her years in Richmond. "The invaluable years of the *Afro* and the *Richmond Free Press* remain forever ingrained in my journalistic DNA."

The *Richmond Voice* and its partner, the *Hampton Roads VOICE*, is currently one of the largest black-oriented community newspaper companies also carrying the heritage of the *Afro-American* in Virginia. Founded in 1986 and located as of 2013 only one block down from the former *Afro-American* location at 205 East Clay Street, the weekly *Voice* Newspaper specializes in minority news coverage specifically in Richmond and the Tidewater area of Virginia. Both papers are distributed free of charge to more than five hundred locations in the Richmond and Hampton Roads metro areas.

Founded as the *Richmond Defender* in February 2005, the *Virginia Defender* is a statewide community newspaper that also carries the legacy passed down from the *Afro-American*. It is published quarterly by "The Defenders for Freedom, Justice and Equality" and headed by Ana Edwards and Phil Wilayto "in the Spirit of Gabriel & Nan, Nat Turner, John Brown, Mary Bowser, Elizabeth Van Lew, John Mitchell Jr., Barbara Johns, Oliver Hill & all who struggle for Justice." The *Defender*'s editorial focus is with "the challenges and the struggles of the working poor, with emphasis on the African-American community," according to Phil Wilayto. The *Defender* is distributed in thirteen cities and three counties in Virginia, plus in Washington, D.C.; North and South Carolina; West Virginia; Utah; and even Tehran, Iran.

THE SUNFLOWER, 1967–1968

The Sunflower *is the local "underground" newspaper put out by the small contingent of wacky and unwashed hippies in Richmond...*[it] *is a sloppy, semi-literate and frequently incoherent tabloid containing a lot of rather boring and illogical articles and poems on Vietnam, narcotics, the new left and flower power.*
—*"Vice Squad Overkill," editorial,* Richmond Times Dispatch,
February 8, 1968

Following the civil rights movement and the dissolution of Edward H. Peeples's news sheet *The Ghost* in 1961, Richmond experienced a six-year drought in underground print media options, despite the slow simmering of a national New Left movement nourished by a number of remarkable events coalescing into what is known today as "the '60s." In June 1962, student activists calling themselves Students for a Democratic Society (SDS) led by Tom Hayden met in Port Huron, Michigan, to draft what became known as the Port Huron Statement, a twenty-five-thousand-word blueprint for the upcoming new era of activism.

"We are people of this generation, bred in at least modest comfort, housed now in universities, looking uncomfortably to the world we inherit," the statement began. "As we grew, however, our comfort was penetrated by events too troubling to dismiss. First, the permeating and victimizing fact of human degradation, symbolized by the Southern struggle against racial bigotry, compelled most of us from silence to activism. Second, the enclosing fact of the Cold War, symbolized by the presence of the Bomb, brought

The Sunflower, November 19, 1967. Art by Ron Poulos. *Courtesy VCU Cabell Library Special Collections, Richmond, Virginia.*

awareness that we ourselves, and our friends, and millions of abstract 'others' we knew more directly because of our common peril, might die at any time."

In 1964, organizing students paralyzed the USC-Berkeley campus when political activity was banned by university officials, resulting in what became quickly known as the Free Speech movement. That movement started a tidal wave of student protest and activism that spent the rest of the decade rolling east across America. In the next two years, the nation experienced the Harlem and Watts riots, the Selma march, the first anti-Vietnam march on Washington and the first university war sit-ins.

While the South and Richmond especially were slower in embracing many more radical aspects of the growing New Left activist movement, the avant-garde art and poetry talents around the RPI and Fan communities were in full swing. As in the '50s, the Village Restaurant remained a centralized hangout for the Beats, leftists, artists and poets, thanks in no small part to the forgiving owners and servers who appreciated the talents and tolerated the poverty of their creative clientele—but only up to a point. "You had to behave. They wouldn't put up with unnecessary shenanigans," said Richmond native Bill Creekmur. "I saw Steve [Dikos] more than once grab somebody by the collar and the belt and walk them right out the door like a battering ram."

In 1963, Rodney Bryan opened the Crossroads Coffee House at 1205 West Franklin Street, just a block west of the RPI campus, serving up hot java and offering local musicians a chance to show their chops.

"For ten years there have been remarkable people creating remarkable myths in Richmond," wrote Fan poet Lester Blackiston. "At the very center of the region/province/city is the 'Fan District,' and the 'Fan' is home to the mythmakers of the last decade—and now, the Fan is daily becoming home to another phenomenon, a remarkable community of numerous individuals whose apparent intentions are to set in motion a pattern of artistic and spiritual consequences. These are the seeds of the garden, and it appears that spring is not far away."

The personalities of the 800 and 900 blocks of West Grace Street especially blossomed during this formative time. Along with the Village, Eton's, Meadow Laundry, the Pink Rhinoceros, Luigi's, SanDors Bookstore and Dutch's Restaurant, the Lee Theater, located at 934 West Grace Street, was an early asset to the RPI and Fan communities. The Lee experimented with a new concept in Richmond theater presentations, showing foreign films, adaptations of operas, ballets or art in any form, and it became known in the late 1950s the "theater of fine art films."

After closing for a brief period, the Lee reopened on Christmas Day 1959. The resurrection was short-lived, as in 1962, the Lee again closed because, as the *Richmond Times Dispatch* lamented, "It is, indeed, a pity if, in a metropolitan area with more than 400,000 residents, there are not enough theater-goers to appreciate good films." The article concluded, "If Bridgett Bardot had made enough pictures, the Lee would still be open."

Not to be held down, the Lee indeed reopened in 1965 with X-rated films and adult-only midnight shows. Although the theater survived several raids and being hauled into courts on obscenity charges, it could not survive the VHS revolution and closed its doors for good in 1983. The former "Lee Art" is now the Grace Street Theater, operated by the VCU theater department.

Roy Scherer recalled his introduction to Grace Street, the Fan and the burgeoning Richmond counterculture upon his arrival in Richmond in late 1964. "I got back in Richmond, bought a motorcycle and started hanging around the Fan," he said. "Walking down the street toward the Village Restaurant, some guy said to me, 'Say can you tell me where Grant's Tomb is?' There really was such a place, down near Laurel and Grace Street. I was amazed; they had some really fun people there."

Howard Fisher opened Grant's Tomb at 802 West Grace Street in early 1967, two doors down from the Richmond headquarters of the Confederate Angels motorcycle gang. "Grant's Tomb was a coffee shop in the back and a one-room store in the front that sold hippie paraphernalia," said artist Mac McWilliams, who worked there in 1967 and '68. "I had a studio pad above the store. Howard rented out several rooms. The coffee shop had barrels for tables and a platform stage. I remember Duck Baker playing there. Rik Davis read poetry there."

As was typical in some larger southern urban areas, the hybrid Beat/hippie presence of Grant's Tomb rubbed some more traditional locals the wrong way. "We often got bricks tossed through the front window when we had a Ho Chi Minh poster hanging there," said McWilliams. "Once we were invaded by three rednecks, who started beating on Howard and breaking up the place. But there was a short hippie ex-marine who ran down from upstairs and plunged a pair of scissors into the main perp's gut. They ran out."

According to an eyewitness, police officers called to investigate the incident placed blame on Fisher, implying that the three "rednecks" had been lured into the place and then beaten without provocation. One even said that the Tomb's business license could be revoked if trouble kept happening there. A second bust on May 25, 1968, for alleged narcotics trafficking yielded only some tea bags and mint leaves, which were confiscated. That anonymous witness also stated, "Police were in rare form as they conducted the search. I heard one say 'Be there, goddammit, be there!' as he searched. Unfortunately, he left disappointed."

Across the road on Laurel Street, Tak and Holly Keck opened and ran the Scarlet Griffin coffee house and bookshop for a brief period. RPI artist Michael Kaluta first pinned his comic *The Eyes of Mars* up on a corkboard inside the Griffin, where it was seen by fellow artist Michael Cody, who passed it along to writer, publisher and comics fan Tom Long. Long included Kaluta in his groundbreaking comics journal *Graphic Showcase*, giving Kaluta his first break in the comics world.

"I spent many enchanting evenings at the Scarlet Griffin as a goggle-eyed freshman art student," said artist Phil Trumbo, "sipping cider, listening to Duck [Baker], John Basset, various blues and jug bands, hanging out at the sandal shop in the basement, the bookstore and studying Kaluta's latest installment of *The Eyes of Mars* comic strip. It was bohemian central."

"We were actually fun-loving hippies," said musician John Harbaugh of the people who hung around Grant's Tomb and the Griffin. "We weren't really radicals, we didn't burn draft cards. We were really kind of poseurs."

Of course, as in the larger cities, drugs played a role in the counterculture at that time. "When Grant's Tomb closed, it became a head shop," said Harbaugh. "Marijuana was big in 1967; LSD was huge, then hash, then when heroin came, everything kind of turned ugly."

"[Richmond's] drug scene started out as very experimental, mostly marijuana," said Richmond native Chuck Wrenn. "I never saw anything until I was in college, around 1967 or so. It was basically kids experimenting with smoking pot; nobody had tried it before. Then, of course, acid came in later, and then the light shows and all that came along. I'm sure there was heroin, but I never saw it. The people I was hanging around with were more about mind expansion, and heroin just did not fit into any of that. Personally, I never wanted anything to do with it."

"It was in Richmond that I first took LSD," said former *Richmond Chronicle* editor Nina Sabaroff (now Katya Sabaroff Taylor). "Homer [Hurst] and I walked to Maymont Park, and I had a religious experience with a seal who poked his eye through a chain link fence to look into mine."

Whether they were fun-loving, pot-smoking "wacky and unwashed hippies," poseurs or even heroin-abusing radicals, RPI poet and artistic entrepreneur Walter "Art" Dorow apparently saw dollar signs in the gathering counterculture storm clouds, so in September 1967, he gathered

The Sunflower,
March 7, 1968.
Art by "Cheese
Enterprises."
*Courtesy Special
Collections, University
of Virginia Library,
Charlottesville,
Virginia.*

several of those people together in an office next door to Grant's Tomb and created volume 1, number 1 of Richmond's own authentic underground newspaper, *The Sunflower.*

"Art Dorow had a love of advertising, music and publishing," said Harbaugh. "But he was an enigma." Some saw Dorow's enigmatic objectives as less than honorable. "He was a hippie, hustler, ad man kind of guy," said artist Terry Rea. "Dorow was a perfect example of a kind of guy who had an eye for style, and could imitate, and he saw the hippie thing and all the crazy graphics of the underground cartoonists, and he figured like most ad men of how find some way to cash in on it—and that I bet was his interest in *The Sunflower.*"

Whatever Dorow's true intentions, the 1960s underground press—in Richmond and across America—was all about reaching out to the people who opposed establishment values and who distrusted and even wholly rejected the conventional media outlets. The impact of alternative news sources and their embrace of nonobjective advocacy reporting from the mid-1960s through the end of the decade defined the way America viewed the massive socioeconomic changes that swept the country during those transformational years. The underground papers considered their unique form of journalism as much creative nonfiction literature as they did communication, conveying their own unique meaning and analysis rather than just information.

Locally, the established media—including the daily newspapers, the TV and radio stations and especially the city government and police department—along with Richmond's white and well-heeled old money population saw the underground and hippie movements creeping into the capital of the Confederacy as immoral and obscene at best, and Marxism bent on government overthrow at worst. Richmond city councilman (and later mayor) Phil Bagley Jr. in a September 25, 1967 *Richmond Times Dispatch* article described hippies as "barefooted, filthy slobs" who created a nuisance and should not be allowed to "conduct their unorthodox activities" in city parks and facilities—a charge that drew a swift rebuttal from fellow councilman Howard Carwile and even the *Richmond Times Dispatch* editorial page.

"Hippies, as a group, are a repulsive, unattractive lot, and Councilman Bagley's aversion to them is understandable," read an October 2, 1967 editorial. "But constitutional guarantees apply even to these off-beat young men and women—many of whom, we venture to predict, will grow up to be conservative-minded adults. Some of them may actually vote Republican."

In the October 10, 1967 edition, columnist Ed Grimsley wrote of an imaginary conversation with a "hippie" he supposedly found "lounging under a tree in Bryant Park, stroking his beard." When asked by Grimsley how he planned to solve the world's problems, the hippie responded "by smoking pot and eating LSD and keeping myself in a hallucinated state…I also refuse to bathe, shave, study or obey any law that displeases. The very idea of work is repulsive and I don't like to wear shoes."

"The Fan was the progressive underground of Richmond—it was like the circus," said Chuck Wrenn. "People would ride through just to look at the hippies. Rednecks would drive through and want to start fights. I think a lot of the west end people looked at it as a bunch of crazy people down there, weirdos, art students. They were kind of afraid of it. People are always afraid of what they don't understand."

In an undated news clipping from around that time headlined "A Mild Form of Hippie Evening," befuddled *Richmond News-Leader* critic Ross Mackenzie (who went on to become a conservative op-ed columnist) tried to describe a music and light show at the "South's finest Ballroom," Richmond's Tantilla Gardens, formerly located at Hamilton and Broad Streets, featuring the Actual Mushroom, Richmond's first psychedelic band:

> *Most intriguing were the 1,000 Richmond Teeny-boppers who allegedly danced to the clanging beat of the Actual Mushroom. They looked more like oysters squirming out of their shells, worms with arms, jumping beans on an oily floor, a revival of snake-hipping aborigines. They dressed in body paint, mini-minis, pajamas, dirty jeans, pith helmets, togas, bell-bottomed trousers and sarongs....Frequently one could not tell which persons represented which sex. The Wan look prevailed.*

Underground newspapers in mid-1967 were still a national novelty but quickly gaining strength in numbers. The culturally significant events of the '60s required a culturally unique medium to report and analyze them, which led to their creation. "The [mainstream] press is losing its power to report spontaneous events," poet Allen Katzman said in 1969. "But it's gaining a new power—to create events; to turn news gathering into news making. The papers of pseudo events, news leaks and press releases offend no one; they take no moral stand. They are just neutral. They furnish our boring and repetitive lives with boring and repetitive 'news.'"

Groups of enterprising young people, buoyed by new cheap printing technologies and united by their inherent distrust of the mainstream media, first banded together in Los Angeles; Berkeley; Lansing and Detroit, Michigan; and New York City to reach out to those like themselves who opposed those commonly accepted establishment values and wished to take advantage of those advances. Their wholesale rejection of the conventional media created what became known as the underground press.

The Underground Press Syndicate (UPS), a coalition of underground papers, listed only eleven such papers in the United States in the winter of 1966. By the time *The Sunflower* published its first issue, there were about twenty-six underground papers listed with the UPS, with only three on the East Coast: *Underground* in Arlington, Virginia; the *East Village Other* in New York City; and *The Eagle* in Washington, D.C. But more were quickly

The Sunflower, volume 1, number 1, November 5, 1967. Art by Dale Milford. *Courtesy John Harbaugh.*

introducing themselves to a public hungry for more nonmainstream news and information, and UPS membership peaked in 1969 with four hundred papers, including eleven from Canada and twenty-three from Europe.

"Given a new youth, a new bohemia, a new iconoclastic humor, a new sexuality, a new sound, a new turn-on, a new abolitionism, a new left, a new hope and a new cynicism, a new press was inevitable," wrote Jacob Brackman in the August 1967 issue of *Playboy* magazine.

The first issue of *The Sunflower* was ten groovy pages of free-flowing visuals never before seen by Richmond and its established "dinosaur media." Coming out on the heels of San Francisco's summer of love, the content of the magazine was decidedly more mellow than aggressive, featuring freestanding art, poetry, essays and news "published by the Sunflower Press, PO drawer 12165, Richmond VA, 23220."

"*The Sunflower* was a homespun type of operation, but it was patterned after those bigger papers like the *Village Voice*, and *Avatar* and *East Village Other*," said Wrenn.

There were very few photographs in the early issues—decorative illustrations by artists John Poulos, Ron Courtney, Chuck Wrenn and Ray Simone swooped and weaved in and out of the IBM Selectrix–produced texts, merging pages into individual works of art much in the way of more established West Coast papers such as San Francisco's visually spectacular but short-lived *Oracle*.

The Sunflower was the ideal vehicle to publicize the spreading counterculture/alternative sentiment and the visible hippie community emerging in Richmond's Fan District. Kicking off the debut issue, Rance Conley wrote in an article oddly titled "Hippiedom, Ism, Ability" that the paper "will examine the salient features of the love generation, with emphasis on those values applicable to the community which the *Sunflower* serves." He concluded the piece, "I'll do my thing and you do yours, but if my revelation turns out to be a lifetime at Reynolds and a home in Bon Air, our mutual love may need some trussing up."

The cover was a freestanding Aztec-style illustration by artist Dale Milford that gave only a subtle hint of what was inside, which included a four-part essay by Jim Warner about Mexico City, "Hot and Cold Culture," that is a fascinating and poetic look at his apparent visit to Mexico's capital city. The unfortunate layout, however, with the typed text wrapping at angles and diagonally around the copious illustrations, made for a difficult read: "An ugly-beautiful world of question-like children in the act of being unquestionable, of multi-colored slums in multi-colored buildings that proclaim in brocade silence the texture of ancient Aztecas though rooms are filled with Bauhaus dreams and stacks of Tanguy's furniture; a nineteen-fortyish world of honky-tonk and pinball machines run head-on into the feudal age."

Pages 4 and 5 featured an angry article by Lester Blackiston, titled "A Three Part Article or Bust," about the growing use of pot and the Richmond penalties attached to smoking. He warned in all caps, "IF YOU DON'T KNOW THE DIFFERENCE BETWEEN THE GREAT PUMPKIN AND THE GREAT COP YOU'RE GOING TO SPEND HALLOWEEN IN THE SNAKE PIT ON FAIRFIELD AVENUE THAT IS CALLED CITY JAIL!"

He went on to offer some "stay safe" axioms to keep the budding pot user out of the Fairfield Avenue snake pit: don't smoke with strangers; smoke in a different place when possible (if you turn on in a group, alternate pads); never discuss even the vaguest details about drugs on the telephone; and finally, "never, no matter how happy you are when he comes to collect, turn on the newspaper boy."

Page 5 of *The Sunflower* included ads by several Richmond businesses eager apparently to support Richmond's entry into the Haight-Ashbury-lite ethos that was blooming in the aristocratic South. Kambourian & Sons, the Village, Dutch's Restaurant and Meadow laundry all bought ad space. The Bosom Blues Band—with light effects by Airflow—advertised also as "now available."

"Airflow was not technically as sophisticated as those big ones but we did it for Springsteen and the 5th Dimension," said Chuck Wrenn. "It was real popular at the time."

Page 7 included the first topical "news" story, titled "Love Without Electricity," about Richmond's supposed first "be-in" (technically not the first; a be-in actually occurred at RPI's Shafer Court on April 25, 1967 to kick off the Bang 4 Art Festival). "Be-ins" started in San Francisco the previous January when the *San Francisco Oracle* called for "A Gathering of the Tribes for a Human Be-In." It was a peaceful, loosely planned gathering of almost fifteen thousand people near the Haight-Ashbury neighborhood that was watched by curious tourists and resulted in not one arrest, despite the attendance of activist Jerry Rubin (fresh out of a Berkeley jail) and Timothy Leary, who first told attendees to "turn on, tune in and drop out."

"Ins" were quite popular in the 1960s: civil rights movements had sit-ins as far back as 1960, and college campuses had teach-ins, so the hippies created be-ins and love-ins. Soon NBC television coopted the term, premiering *Rowan and Martin's Laugh-In* in January 1968.

An estimated two thousand people gathered on a cloudy September Saturday in Richmond's Forest Hill Park to hear poetry and "electric music" by local musicians, but it was discovered thirty minutes before show time that the generator brought to provide electricity was DC, not AC, and therefore worthless. An attempt was made to plug an extension cord into the public washroom, but the city shut off the current. When one kindly neighbor allowed the "hippies" to plug in for fifteen dollars, city police showed up and informed the be-in planners that there was no way they were going to string one hundred yards of extension cords through trees and across the road, an edict that put a premature end to the gathering. "The people wrapped up the extension cords, acknowledging defeat at the hands of the uniformed representatives of the power structure," *The Sunflower* noted. "They went back to the thousand people, gathered to hear electric music, and told them there would be no juice."

Still, as the article concluded, "even without juice there had been a lot of communication…people got together, met each other, enjoyed the day and the park…The police got a shot at the visible hippie community. Nice."

"In one of your recent articles, I read that Richmond was allegedly free of hippies," wrote Mrs. Bryan Bowers in an October 1 letter to the *Times Dispatch* editor. "Last Sunday at Forest Hill Park seemed to prove otherwise. The happy people who filled the park spent the day visiting, singing, listening and romping…I am tired of reading detrimental remarks directed against hippies—I, for one, are for them!" Not declaring defeat, the Richmond be-in organizers planned another "Electric Be-In" in Monroe Park, featuring the Bosom Blues Band.

"I was involved [with *The Sunflower*] only on the periphery," said South Carolina artist John Poulos, whose name appeared on a chaotic cover collage for volume 1, number 2, which featured among other things naked females complete with visible pubic hair ("Looks like five or six different photocopies from different pages!" Poulos said when he saw the cover for the first time in 2012). "As I recall, Art or someone on his staff asked me for artwork. I gave them a sketchbook; they chopped it up like with a hatchet. I did one or two comic strips, ducked into Art's creepy, dark apartment only once, saw only one or two issues, then got fired for a lack of revolutionary, militant fervor."

As for whether the staff of *The Sunflower* was militant, Poulos said, "I think they were actually pretty docile all in all, with maybe only a couple of loose cannons roaming the decks. I distinctly remember someone flipping open his Korean-era U.S. Army field jacket and showing me a hand grenade hanging there, with some talk of the SDS and their dissatisfaction with my sense of humor."

With a biweekly publication schedule, rented office space and the accompanying expenses associated with publishing, *The Sunflower* sold for twenty-five cents per issue, utilizing (like almost every other underground magazine nationwide) commissioned salespeople to hawk the magazines on street corners.

"They would front you papers, then you would go out and sell them retail and come back and pay for them wholesale," said Roy Scherer. "If they didn't know you, they wouldn't front you very many papers…once you had a track record with them, they would front you a bunch."

This method was slightly different than the West Coast papers like the *Berkeley Barb*, which made their vendors purchase the papers wholesale at fifteen cents per copy then sell them for twenty-five cents, allowing them to pocket the dime profit.

"Most of the people sold right around RPI," said Scherer. "A few people would sell them out at University of Richmond, but I took them downtown. I'd sell four or five to people going to work in the morning, then at lunchtime, I would sell fifteen or twenty. Then at quitting time, I'd sell a shitload. Made a significant amount of money doing that."

John Harbaugh said that in 1968 he took a bundle to D.C., and they sold well. Was he harassed by the police? "Yea, the cops would say, 'Move along,' then I would walk down the block then come right back."

"I would sell *The Sunflower*, but I didn't write for it," recalled Chuck Wrenn. "I would sell them on the street newsboy style on the corner by the Village. One time, Lynn Abbott had written a piece that used the word 'fuck.' I got arrested and charged with selling obscene literature because of that word. The ACLU got involved, and they said before I could be charged with selling obscene literature, they had to prove in a court of law that it is an obscene word before I could be charged. They didn't want any part of that. They dropped it. Dorow and Abbot went down and got me out, and I wrote an article about the arrest."

Wrenn was arrested shortly before midnight February 5, 1968, by vice cops who came into his apartment, woke him up, dumped everything on the floor and confiscated copies of the allegedly obscene issue. The arrest and the way it was conducted received a short but intense burst of mainstream media coverage. "The local radio stations sent the electrifying news sizzling over the airwaves every hour on the hour," noted an uncredited story in *The Sunflower*. "The *Cheese Leader* ran the facts (in good taste, of course), the *Times Disgrace* did their version of the other version, and even the *Proscript* did a student version of the morning version of the evening version. Information saturation soaked into the pores of every red white and blue blooded obscenity hating American in Richmond."

Two days later, an editorial in the *Richmond Times Dispatch* actually chided the vice division for the middle-of-the-night arrest and defended Wrenn and *The Sunflower*, albeit in a backhanded manner: "Obnoxious? Yes. Objectionable? By all means. But obscene? Not in terms of current legal standards and recent court rulings." "We find it highly significant," the editorial continued, "...that the Episcopal book store, of all places, not only has been selling the *Sunflower* (including the particular issue charged with being obscene) but it also supports the publication with its advertising. If the vice squad really thought it had a case, perhaps it was an oversight that, instead of rousting a 22-year-old RPI student out of his apartment at midnight, it didn't break into the Episcopal book store to arrest the nice little lady who has been peddling the same allegedly 'obscene' literature from behind her desk."

Two weeks prior to Wrenn's arrest, Art Dorow and Rance Conley were invited to the University of Richmond by the Canterbury Club to meet with students about the "hippie" movement. According to the February 2, 1968 *Collegian*, Conley told the gathered students that "hippie" was a "press label" and that they preferred to call their movement the "culture," as opposed to the "establishment."

"The establishment will provide three squares a day," Conley said, "but some people are looking for more in the business world."

Sometime in 1968, *The Sunflower* joined the Underground Press Syndicate and subscribed to the Liberation News Service (LNS). The LNS was a Washington, D.C.–based national news service like the Associated Press but designed exclusively for the counterculture and underground scene (although several "aboveground" papers such as the *Village Voice* also subscribed). It was originally started and operated by two eccentric young men named Raymond Mungo and Marshall Bloom who had been trying to run and radicalize the United States Student Press Association. In a 2000 e-mail to Katya Sabaroff Taylor, Mungo said that "Marshall Bloom was in fact the real father of the LNS...Barbara Heimlich and I followed him out the door of the U.S. Student Press Association, and we set up LNS shop right down the same block of Washington D.C. The house was part news service, part commune, part insane asylum."

Incorporated under the name the New Media Project, the LNS was an attempt at a new kind of journalism—to develop a more personal style of reporting and question established notions of "objectivity." For a fifteen-dollar fee, the subscribing papers and magazines twice a week received a packet of professionally prepared content, including stories, photos and drawings for unlimited use.

"We weren't particularly rigorous journalists," said former LNS member Beryl Epstein in an e-mail, "but more often than not, the 'controversial' stuff that we wrote about was later grudgingly revealed by the establishment media to be pretty close to the mark. It was always nice to get that additional corroboration."

The LNS became the coast-to-coast connecting device needed by the increasingly radical papers. Soon LNS began to attract quality journalists like Thorne Dreyer and the *Washington Post*'s Allen Young, who kept the organization together during a bitter internal rift. By the time LNS moved its headquarters from Washington to New York in the spring of 1968, a talented and diversified group of writers, editors and photographers was providing crucial coverage of some important events with a unique viewpoint, including the 1967 March on the Pentagon and the 1968 Columbia University revolt, where the LNS was the only news outlet to embed reporters inside the university.

"We would gather around a huge table and we would literally have the packets laid out and we would all go in a circle for an hour or two and collate and staple the packets," said former LNS member Katya Sabaroff Taylor in a 2008 interview with underground press historian Blake Slonecker. "It was like slave labor, but you know we were giddy, we were excited, we were laughing. It was great. Then we would go home at three in the morning."

As America slogged through the politically and culturally transformational year of 1968, *The Sunflower* also grew increasingly militant, enthusiastically espousing more and more antiestablishment sentiment, such as college unrest, sexual revolution, exposing police brutality, increasing drug use and exposing the failure of the established media to recognize that times were changing, the "gentle hippie" days were waning and the language of the counterculture was shifting from "protest" to "resistance" to "revolution." The May 9, 1968 *Sunflower* cover included a quote by Che Guevara, and the May 28 issue showed a photo of a group of riot police standing over several young people on the ground—a common sight at almost any hippie gathering.

The Sunflower chronicled Richmond drug arrests at least twice by printing a "Bust Map" showing the locations and dates of all the narcotics arrests, with (surprise) almost all of them occurring in the Fan District between Monroe Park and Boulevard. "Given the fact that ambitious vice-squadsmen now cruise in slick Mustangs and Barracudas, grow long hair and whiskers guaranteed to infiltrate the most hardened potbed of druggies, with any luck at all you might get put on the map this year," the caption sarcastically suggested.

"All the drug searches were done in the Fan—they wanted the hippies and the RPI students," said Wrenn. "I still have two search warrants signed by [vice squad lieutenant] Higgins myself. Higgins searched my apartment twice looking for drugs and never found anything. They would come in and start throwing everything in the middle of the floor, pull your books off the shelf, pull the mattress off the bed, throw it all down, and if they didn't find anything, they would say, 'Well you're lucky—we didn't find anything.' I was a high-profile person at the time, involved with putting on shows and playing with bands myself, so I guess I drew a lot of attention."

"I have lived in Richmond for the past 14 years, since I was six," wrote John English in a letter in the October 9, 1967 *Times Dispatch*, "and I have learned in that time how useless it is to object to police outrages. The department has always harassed young people and most likely always will."

"Lieutenant Higgins frisked me when he burst into my apartment one night for possession of a small amount of cannabis," Karl Waldbauer said in 2013. "I was in bed with my wife and was frisked while completely nude. Higgins swore under oath the tea container holding my pot was found in the water closet of my toilet when, in fact, it was found in a log pile outside my back door."

A thought-provoking photo spread by Marc Harriman in the April 11, 1968 *Sunflower* documented almost wordlessly a spontaneous civil rights demonstration that grew violent downtown the previous Palm Sunday, three days after the assassination of Dr. Martin Luther King Jr., resulting in numerous broken windows and the arrest of Greyhound employee Linwood Corbett. "The record shows that on April 7 at about 1:15 a.m. a large crowd of Negroes had congregated at Third and Broad streets in Richmond," noted the transcript of *Linwood Corbett v. Commonwealth of Virginia*. "Responding to a radio call, Officers Bogart and Shook of the Richmond Police Department arrived at the scene. The officers testified that they observed Appellant standing on an upturned trash can waving his hands and addressing the crowd. The group was 'noisy,' but others appeared to be trying to listen to Corbett."

"I got up with a desire in my heart to try to do something constructive, not destructive," testified Corbett, who was charged with unlawful assembly and disturbing the peace. "My only intentions were to tell the people if you are going to be here demonstrate in a more orderly manner." The charges against him were dismissed.

"Plate glass being replaced, the occupying army out in force. What's wrong with these people?" the cryptic extended caption in *The Sunflower* pleaded. "Why do they burn and loot and destroy? Don't they realize everything's all right? Or could it be that everything isn't all right, and no one's doing anything about it."

Dr. King was supposed to be in Richmond for the "Poor Peoples" campaign on April 7, but he canceled his Virginia tour to instead stay and support the Memphis sanitation worker strike—a decision that cost him his life. "He would have been speaking at [Sixth Mount Zion Baptist Church] on Duval Street, and we were prepared," former ABC store manager Daniel Perkins told *The Voice* newspaper in 1991. "We had Black officers that were going to be ushers, even singing in the choir."

On the day King was murdered, boxer Muhammad Ali was in Richmond speaking to a group of Virginia Union students. "I heard Muhammad Ali at Virginia Union today," *Richmond Afro-American* writer Barry Barkan told *The Sunflower*, "and I got so excited I wanted to give up my slave name, and I'm *white*."

Meanwhile, over on the VCU campus, a whole other controversy exploded in October 1968 just as the school attained its coveted university status. The student newspaper *Proscript* erroneously reported that the newest way to protest the Vietnam War was scheduled for the following Tuesday by the Students for Liberal Government (SLG) in a happening entitled "Time Out." Jeffrey Kelso, the organization's student government representative, reportedly asserted that "a live dog would be sacrificed at VCU on a wooden funeral pyre to 'protest the horrors of the war in Vietnam.'"

The rumor of the "puppy burn"—fired by a nebulous metaphor uttered by Kelso at an SGA meeting and spurred by the factually incorrect *Proscript* story—had the anticipated effect. "The Students for Liberal Government are about to hang their organization on an ever-shortening rope of rash ideas," wrote Editor Christy Cooke in the October 18, 1968 issue of the *Proscript*. "Who can assure us that, in the frenzy of mob spirit, the puppy would not be sacrificed? We need only to look at history—the Nazi party, for example—to see that a mob spirit can actually commit the foulest of crimes once a crowd is uncontrollable."

"Someone mailed a copy of the story to [Jeff's] parents," said Roy Scherer, "and the *Times Dispatch* and the *News-Leader* picked up on the story, so did the TV and the radio…and [Jeff] said, 'We have a permit, we haven't broken any laws,' without revealing any other details."

Of course it was a hoax. A Student Government committee studied the "puppy burn," and Acting Provost Francis J. Brooke released a statement October 25 stating, in part, that "no puppy has been burned, and the administration has been repeatedly assured by numerous students that no students intend now, nor had they ever intended, to engage in any act of cruelty to any animal."

Once exposed, the *Proscript* had to issue a part retraction, part apology titled "Comedy of Errors": "We sincerely regret the action that was attributed to the Students for Liberal Government...We should have realized the act was a cheap publicity stunt."

Still, on that fateful "Time Out" on October 29, about five hundred students and an untold number of police, animal rights activists, FBI agents, probably undercover CIA agents and even members of the KKK gathered in Monroe Park to hear speeches by SLG reps and those of national student groups. No dogs were allowed.

"Why are you here?" Kelso asked the crowd to a chorus of boos after arriving. "Not to protest the war in Vietnam—no, you are here today to protest the alleged destroying of a puppy...Right now, there is a child burning taking place in Vietnam." Also speaking at that rally was Dave Hawk of the National Students' Association and *Afro-American* reporter Barry Barkan, who invited hecklers to go with him "anytime" to see how poor people live in Richmond. The Nazi-like "frenzy of mob spirit" never materialized, and no puppies were harmed during the rally.

The VCU Board of Visitors stated in a dour manner with no details in its October 31, 1968 special meeting minutes, "At this point, the Rector departed from the prepared Agenda to receive a report from Dr. Charles M. Renneisen, Dean of Students, with respect to the recent 'Puppy Burn' matter...Signed and approved by Mr. Virginius Dabney, Chairman."

It is unknown if *The Sunflower* was even still publishing on a regular basis by then. "I have no idea when or why *The Sunflower* stopped publishing," said Chuck Wrenn, although it most likely folded over money, born by the bad press received after Wrenn's obscenity arrest, as indicated by a house ad in the March 7, 1968 issue: "So, to be quite frank, we are in trouble. Money trouble, that is," the ad noted. "Even though we were cleared of the obscenity charge, it did a good job on us by putting people up tight."

The latest issue found, volume 2, number 1, was published on October 10, 1968. An unidentified woman and Editor Art Dorow, with his hand outstretched, appear on the cover.

Puppy burns, student movements, obscenity and drug busts and agitators aside, Chuck Wrenn agreed that it was the combination of the personality of the Fan District, hippie radicals and the presence of RPI and especially the art school that fed the short but intense history of *The Sunflower*. "In high school I remember the adults saying, 'RPI—where the girls are girls and the boys are too.' We didn't know what we were doing, but we knew we wanted to be a part of it."

Is there still a counterculture in Richmond?

"Gosh, I hope so."

THE *RICHMOND CHRONICLE* AND *PHASE ONE*, 1969–1971

I think all underground papers faced the dilemma of "feeding" the consciousness of those already converted to "our" way of thinking, while also upgrading the consciousness of those who had yet to "see the light."
—*former* Richmond Chronicle *editor Nina Sabaroff (now Katya Sabaroff Taylor), 2012*

There was nothing vulgar or obscene about the Richmond Chronicle, *but it had a lot of weird ideas.*
—*Virginia Beach Municipal court judge P.B. White, quoted in a* Richmond Times Dispatch *story "Newsboy Arrested at Beach," September 16, 1969*

In late 1967, a new experiment in learning called "Free University" began appearing in various cities across the United States, both as freestanding institutions and extensions of existing urban universities. The first Free University, on the USC-Berkeley campus, grew out of the Free Speech movement and spread mostly to other west coast, midwest and northern state campuses.

Free universities offered subjects that were based solely on student interest and not part of any formal university curriculum. They had no accreditation, gave no grades, charged minimal or no fees and had no formal faculty members. Michael Kindman wrote of the Free University in his 1966 paper "The Rites/Rights of Spring" that they were "an alternative to the drab, automated education of course outlines, credits, multiple-choice exams and

Richmond Chronicle, June 1, 1970. *Courtesy Alderman Library, University of Virginia, Charlottesville, Virginia.*

IBM cards." By 1971, there were about 110 Free Universities across the United States.

In September 1969, the VCU Students for Liberal Government received a $2,275 grant from the Student Government contingency fund to form its own Free University, headquartered at 725 West Broad Street in Richmond. The scheduled courses listed in the first fall bulletin included Hypnosis, Creativity, Blues Guitar Workshop, Emotional Hang-ups, Poetry, Theater, Print Shop and Photography. The bulletin also stated that anyone who wanted to organize a class could do so. All classes started at 7:00 p.m., so as not to interfere with students' "drab, automated education" during the day.

Richmond's Free University was designed not just as a selection of night classes but as a (counter)cultural immersion—there is even an unconfirmed rumor that students met for one class nude. Any Richmond resident could take any class for two dollars or purchase a "red card" for twenty dollars that included overall registration to as many classes as desired, twelve admissions to the Friday and Saturday night performances at the Performing Arts Center at 313 North Laurel Street and admission to five of the twelve FU-sponsored films, which included the John Lennon film *How I Won the War* and Norman McLaren's indie film *McLaren's Wild Objects*, among others.

Although many Free University classes in urban areas were heavily leftist politically, Richmond's FU chose to remain politically neutral, offering courses that were mostly craft or skill oriented, with a few focused on interpersonal awareness. Classes met wherever they could find space; Reid Cornwell's class on emotional hang-ups was featured in an undated *Richmond Times Dispatch* clipping, showing a handful of (dressed) students in a small, spartan room seated on makeshift benches and even on the floor. A lit cigarette can be seen in Cornwell's hand while he teaches.

Richmond poet Rik Davis taught a poetry class at Free University while he was a sophomore English major at VCU. "I have enough of a sense of commitment to the community to repay for the good things they've provided me: fellowship, friendship, and so forth," he told the October 9, 1969 issue of the *Commonwealth Times*. The article went on to state that Davis had "in addition to his duties at VCU, over 30 volumes of prose to his credit," without clarifying that most if not all of those volumes were pulp pornographic novels, written for such publishers as Satan Books, under the pseudonym Jack Vast.

By March 1970, Free University had ceased operations, citing a general lack of interest and a standing debt of about $2,200. A concert with a band

Richmond Chronicle, April 1, 1970. *Courtesy Special Collections, University of Virginia Library, Charlottesville, Virginia.*

called Steel Mill (featuring a long-haired guitarist named Bruce Springsteen) and a rummage sale secured enough funds to pay off the debt, with a little left over to help fund the recently formed Radical Student Union.

The main reason for the debt, according to the March 4, 1970 issue of the *Commonwealth Times*, was the publication of Free University's own tabloid news magazine, the *Richmond Chronicle*. The *Chronicle* absorbed $1,400 of the original $2,275 funded by the VCU SGA, leaving little money to fund learning space and make necessary infrastructural improvements to the buildings and classrooms.

The *Richmond Chronicle* was originally published biweekly as an "independent free press" publication, with single copies originally costing fifteen cents (but bumped up to twenty-five cents with issue number 3 so street vendors could "support themselves" selling it). The first issue was published early in the summer of 1969, a few months before the start of the Free University academic year, predating the debut issue of VCU's "official" school newspaper, the *Commonwealth Times*.

The *Chronicle* was not named in honor of the 1795 Richmond broadsheet of the same name. "We decided to call it the *Chronicle* because that name indicated a more serious approach to news and information than *The Sunflower*, which was a beautifully done alternative 'culture' paper," said cofounder and former editor Bruce Smith. "I chose the name when the *San Francisco Chronicle* came to my mind as a serious, somewhat progressive paper."

A native Virginian, Smith attended Lynchburg College and in 1964 was a founding member of the Southern Students Organizing Committee (SSOC), a student-led antiracist membership organization that was in alliance with black organizations, such as the Black Panthers, to challenge what they perceived in the United States to be a white supremacist socioeconomic system. Smith moved to Richmond in 1968 after working to organize SSOC chapters at Virginia Tech and University of Virginia, where he eventually caught the attention of the FBI, which likened the SSOC to the much more radical SDS. Fellow coeditor Lynn Abbott is also a Richmond native and *Sunflower* alumnus. He attended Randolph-Macon College in Ashland as an English major before transferring to VCU.

"Bruce was like the traveling activist," said Chuck Wrenn. "He came in with the beret and the turtleneck, and he was hooked up with all the radical groups. He looked the part and was all about it."

Part of Smith's role in the SSOC was to educate students and their communities' attitudes toward the growing civil rights movement and to bring a closer understanding and working relationship between the students' mostly white middle-class background with working-class whites and people of color. "Now is the time for us to turn inward, toward middle class, white society," Smith told a group of Virginia Tech students at an SSOC gathering in July 1968, as reported in *Alice*, a Blacksburg-based underground tabloid. "This is not the time to be burying our heads in the sand and 'grooving on our own thing' while our neighbors fearfully arm themselves against the Yellow and Black hordes about to invade their suburban sanctuaries. This is the time to get into our communities and find out what makes them tick, and why our friends are afraid."

By summer 1969, the communal, peace-loving flower children of 1967 Richmond were morphing into more socially militant, social justice–driven radicals, angry about Nixon, poverty, racial injustice and Vietnam; fed up with institutionalized higher education, a condescending mainstream media and thuggish police tactics; and prepared to confront and overthrow the various "power structures" that they found so confining. "In July of 1969, Jim Lee Scott [a fellow SSOC activist] and I drove to Berkley and Oakland, California to attend the [Black Panther–sponsored] National Conference to Combat Fascism," said Smith. "We came away solidly in support of the Panthers, less so of the Communist Party and disgusted by the conduct of some white radicals associated with SDS, particularly those associated with Progressive Labor and the Weathermen."

Unlike its predecessor *The Sunflower*, which with exceptions reflected a more placid cultural and social consciousness despite the radical proclivities of many of its staff, the *Richmond Chronicle* was a much more hard-hitting news publication, broadcasting those post-hippie social alarms and reporting not just the travails of the impoverished and unprotected but also the brick- and rock-throwing exploits of those fed up with societal norms and ready to initiate major change. These people were not poseurs; they were serious.

Prior to his involvement with the *Chronicle*, Smith located a Richmond-area print shop that agreed to print an antiwar underground GI paper called *Bragg Briefs*, which was written by and for soldiers at Fort Bragg, North Carolina, where his former roommate and early *Chronicle* coeditor, the late Bob Foley, was sent to boot camp after being drafted in 1968. "They put together the paper, sent it to me in Richmond, where it was printed, and I took it back to them in Fayetteville, where it was distributed," said Smith. "The army thought Foley was responsible but couldn't pin it on him because he never touched it. When he got out of Basic, he was sent to Fort Lee, where he began to work with me and the *Chronicle* on weekends and nights."

As a pre-draft graduate student, Foley had also worked on the Dallas, Texas–based paper *Notes from the Underground*. "He brought a more serious sense of underground media to Richmond," said Smith.

"The purpose of the *Chronicle* is to report news that is ignored or blacked out by the conventional press," cofounder Lynn Abbott said in an October 1969 *Commonwealth Times* interview, repeating the aspirations (and business model) of most countercultural and underground newspapers in existence at that time and barely hinting at the radicalism stewing beneath those words. "All aspects of the paper are to serve the people rather than a 'power structure.'" According to Abbott, the *Chronicle* was already in the "thinking stages" when Free University was formed since *The Sunflower* ceased publication. "It was obvious we were forming a community, and the community needed a mouthpiece."

In addition to local news, the *Chronicle* featured copy from the Liberation News Service, social commentary, record and book reviews, poetry, short fiction and original artwork. It averaged about sixteen pages per edition. Like *The Sunflower*, the *Chronicle* also quickly became a member of the Underground Press Syndicate and a subscriber to the LNS.

"I believe that the *Chronicle* staff hoped to support and spur activism among white and black folks by reporting stories of abuse by powerful people and the authorities and stories of resistance to that abuse," said Smith.

It was Smith's fellow SSOC activists Gene Guerrero and Howard Romaine who founded Atlanta's collectively managed underground newspaper the *Great Speckled Bird* in 1968. Many late 1960s alternative papers wrestled with the complications of "collective" participation within their organizational structure, of giving all staff members equal say in the overall operation and selection of the contributions, regardless of experience. "They were long," Katya Sabaroff Taylor said of the collective-managed LNS meetings she attended before her arrival in Richmond. "They went on endlessly because one of the things about a collective is that everybody gets to say whatever they want to say, and then everybody else gets to answer."

"The *Chronicle* was not published by a collective," wrote Smith. "[The LNS's] Nina Sabaroff was the first Editor of the *Richmond Chronicle*. Bob Foley and I helped get the paper organized and Nina came down to serve as our editor. Then I became Editor after Nina went west." It was also at this time that Bob Foley went to Canada to avoid being sent to Vietnam.

"The editor of the [*Chronicle*] was not interested in dying in Vietnam, so he escaped to Canada, leaving a space for me, who with my LNS 'credentials' seemed next in line for the job," said Sabaroff Taylor, who just happened to be in Richmond at the time because her boyfriend was a VCU art student. "It was thrilling for me because at LNS, I had to work my way up to having some political clout. In Richmond, I was able to step up to the plate and trust my politics and my savvy as a journalist in ways I couldn't have done if I had stayed at LNS."

To Sabaroff Taylor's surprise, it appears she may have been America's first female underground newspaper editor, taking the job in August 1969. "If I was first, then of course you know it was by chance that I happened to show up just when the editor was leaving," she said when informed in 2012 of her honor. "I have no recall of anyone at that time giving me a hard time or challenging my ideas or managerial style because I was a woman."

Abbott went on to claim that the *Chronicle* was not really an "underground" publication; it employed a hardcore group of about a dozen staff members as a permanent staff to make sure the paper got out on time. The staff box in many issues read only "Anybody" or "The People." "In reality there is no 'organizational structure' as such," Lynn Abbott told the *CT* in 1969. "We tried to structure it and we found out people generally do what they want."

"People who were ready to get involved, work hard and become part of something bigger than themselves," said Sabaroff Taylor.

Sabaroff Taylor worked not just as editor but as a prolific writer during her stint in Richmond, penning cover and interior story topics that the daily papers avoided, including those on women's rights, homosexuality, anti-Vietnam protests and the Black Panthers. "The Panthers and the Patriots really did come to town," she wrote in the cover story for the September 15, 1969 issue about a Monroe Park rally for the Black Panthers and the Young Patriots. "It was an historic moment for Richmond, when a group of about 50—cops, FBI agents, a narc or two, a few reporters and media-men, and some Free U people and community passers-by— gathered in Monroe Park Sept. 16 to hear Bob Lee and Preacherman talk about their organizations."

The rally was influential and inspiring to those few in attendance, including herself. "I'm really exhausted," she wrote in a September 17, 1969 personal journal entry. "Didn't sleep all night because I had been so stimulated by Panther B. Lee and Preacherman at the press conference."

"I think [the *Chronicle*] really wanted to have an impact, and hoped we were, in a positive way, raising people's consciousness and getting them involved in social change," she said in 2013. "But of course it was and probably still is somewhat of an uphill battle, because most people are resistant to change and are made uncomfortable when things are pointed

The Richmond Chronicle

VOLUME 1, NUMBER 4 **25 CENTS** **SEPTEMBER 15–30, 1969**

"America has her heel on everyone's neck."

PANTHERS AND PATRIOTS

by Nina Sabaroff

"There's a cancer in Richmond. Whites fight blacks. Blacks fight whites. This gotta stop. Genocide gotta stop. We're headed for a race war. Someone's gotta get up and say 'No good.' Brothers, white and black, you gotta get up off your hind-haunches and get busy."

The Panthers and the Patriots really did come to town. It was an historic moment for Richmond, when a group of about 50 — cops, FBI agents, a narc or two, a few reporters and media-men, and some Free U people and community passers-by — gathered in Monroe Park on Sept. 16 to hear Bob Lee and Preacherman talk about their organizations.

With the Confederate flag (Young Patriot symbol of the right of the people to rebel) and a Black Panther painted on cloth draped behind them, the two Field Secretaries gave a press conference as part of their Southern and Eastern tour to counter heavy oppression against the Panther Party. The two groups hope to set up chapters in the South.

When asked why they had come to Richmond, Panther Bob Lee responded, "We came all the way from Chicago to talk, to stop this bullshit. We know there's a lack of communication... We want to build communication, and we're putting our lives on the line to do that."

He spoke of the national conspiracy to destroy the Black Panther Party, no overstatement when 31 of the Panthers have been shot down since January of this year, and over 400 of them are tied up in jails and courts on trumped-up charges. This includes three of their most charismatic party members: Huey P. Newton, founder of the Party, jailed on a phony manslaughter charge; Eldridge Cleaver, in exile; and Bobby Seale, co-founder of the Party, incarcerated recently on trumped-up murder charges. To show the illegitimacy of charges against the Panthers, Lee cited the instance of the Chicago 16, arrested and held (without bail) on charges of rape. Two of the accused are women.

Lee himself faces charges, "My crime is feeding 4,000 hungry Chicago children each day, providing day-care centers and free health clinics...my crime is serving the people."

The Panthers and Patriots, as well as the Young Lords (a Puerto Rican organization) have formed an alliance known as the Rainbow Coalition. (Both Patriots and the Young Lords are based in Chicago and are ex-street gangs turned revolutionary.) Lee pointed out that this is the first time that blacks, browns, and whites have united their struggles against the oppressor. This should counter, he added, any establishment propaganda about how their organizations are racist. "So when you be a racist when you're a socialist?, Lee asked. "How can you be a racist when you're a revolutionary?"

"We never have been racist," he continued. (The reporters took some notes on this; the cops, in their white shirts, suits and ties, watched from a distance.) "We hate the oppressor no matter what color he is." As for police brutality, the police are public servants. The people pay his taxes. "So when he comes into our community brutalizing us," said Lee, "he's out of order. He's out of order." When he gets out con'd p. 13

Preacher Man, field secretary of the Young Patriots Organization, Chicago's poor white streetgang turned politicos. Right on!

POLICE BRUTALITY

Police brutality was exposed to unbelieving white America during the Democratic Convention in Chicago, when their own sons and daughters were receiving the blunt end of the blackjack. But police brutality didn't start with white yippies, freaks, and radicals — they became "niggers" late. Police brutality in the black ghettos has been around as long as the ghettos, though until recently there's been an almost total news blackout on the harrassment and murder which is a common occurence there.

Now that the press can no longer hide the fact of police brutality to aware Americans white and black, it tries to pass off acts of brutality onto individual, "lax" policemen who, under extreme provocation, occasionally lose the strict and responsible discipline and sense of community service which all policemen normally have.

The news can't be blacked out totally, and the gap is growing between what authorities give out in official releases and in reluctant interviews with the press, and what actually happens on the streets of America. And on the streets of Richmond.

Jo Jo Farmer was seized, handcuffed, and beaten Sept. 1 by Richmond city police. Jo Jo is black and lives in cont. on p. 4

Richmond Chronicle, September 15, 1969. Courtesy Alderman Library, University of Virginia, Charlottesville, Virginia.

out to them they would rather ignore. I'm sure at times we felt exhilarated when things went well and downhearted when we felt like we were spinning our wheels and not really affecting the change we were so longing for."

The *Chronicle* periodically worked with Detroit native Barry Barkan, a reporter for the *Richmond Afro-American* newspaper who helped craft many stories about Richmond residents living under the poverty line, usually with no police protection in altercations. "The best story we carried was based on a community source in which a Richmond narc squad leader was compromised," said Smith.

> *We also received info from community people that Chief of Police [Frank] Duling was making money re-selling confiscated personal property, and the Mayor at the time was the "liquor man," in control of illegal liquor in Richmond. I got that info from a (probably) mafia guy who was visiting Richmond making arrangements for the city not to hassle his employers as he bought four clubs in town in expectation of liquor by the drink going through in the next state legislature. It happened, and I verified the purchase of one of the places when I interviewed one of the employees. We did not report that info but kept it in the memory file as protection against more police harassment.*

Exposing undercover "narcs" was also a mission of the *Chronicle*. Smith related one story where they outed a young woman called "George" in order to spare attacks on her by Fan residents. "Once she was outed, she could not continue with her 'work,'" he said.

Richmond Vice Squad lieutenant Joe Higgins was a frequent target of the *Chronicle*, with unflattering news shorts and even cartoons depicting him as a sneering, corrupt psychopath. Nicknamed "Piggins," he was well known throughout the Fan and VCU communities. "Lt. Joseph Higgins, head of the city vice squad has made his public appearance in the Village, checking I.D.'s just to let all know he still exists," warned a column in the March 3, 1969 VCU Arts Union newsletter. "Oh, yes, my friends, Big Brother is arriving, it is no time for games. Clean up, and most important, stay clean."

Harassment not just by "Piggins" and his vice squad but also by city police and FBI was a legitimate problem for the *Chronicle* staff, as it was for numerous underground and alternative papers across the country. "A decision that many of us made back then was to not record anything we said, did or wrote to friends," Smith said. "We were under attack by right-wing groups and government agents, so it just did not make sense to record things that would assist political persecution. Civilian and military agents were watching, listening and infiltrating our ranks regularly. If this weren't true, it would have been paranoia, but it was a fact."

Smith's suspicions were justified, as police and especially the FBI had these groups and publications under surveillance for years. A Bureau counterintelligence program established in 1968 called COINTELPRO-New Left, which originally had been created as a domestic spying program in 1956, ran an insidious and illegal campaign across the country to disrupt and infiltrate organizations and underground papers considered subversive, including all college newspapers, leftist publications, their staffs, printers and even their funding sources. Declassified documents headed "Disruption of the New Left" obtained through Freedom of Information proved that the SSOC and Smith in particular had been under surveillance by the Richmond FBI Field Office since May 1968.

One COINTELPRO memo from the Richmond "Special Agent in Charge" (SAC) dated November 5, 1968, asked for Bureau authority to distribute anonymous mimeographed bulletins around VCU and the Fan protesting a "hippie paraphernalia" shop on Ryland Street. "It is time for some organization to finally speak out honestly in opposition to the Students for a Democratic Society and Southern Student Organizing Committee and any other new left group of kooks and anti-Americans," the heavily redacted proposed bulletin suggested, "…[t]he most recent example of this is the appearance of a sign in the window of a shop on Ryland Street in Richmond [which] contains four-letter words that are obscene. This shop is in a residential area of elderly people, and passersby who read the sign are shocked and embarrassed." The fake bulletin concludes with the promise that "we hope to keep you informed of the activities of these loud and smelly minorities."

Bruce Smith explained that the store on Ryland Street—called the "Liberated Area"—served as their office, underground newspaper distribution center and as a psychedelic poster and paraphernalia (head) shop. "The novelties include beads, shawls, hats, pins, paper flowers and other items popular with 'hippies,'" said a November 19, 1968 Bureau memo.

Ultimately, however, this idea was rejected by FBI headquarters because it carried an unnecessary "element of risk." "You should review this entire situation for the purpose of developing a program that would result in the closing of Smith's store," noted a November 27 memo from Hoover to the Richmond SAC.

As a result of the harassment instigated by COINTELPRO in conjunction with city governments and local police, including Richmond's, Tom Forcade of the Underground Press Syndicate reported in December 1968 of no fewer than twenty-eight underground papers experiencing harassment and persecution. Atlanta's *Great Speckled Bird* found itself under attack in 1969 from a phantom group called the DeKalb Parents League for Decency, which stated that it was "disturbed" by the "sacrilege, pornography, depravity, immorality, and draft dodging which are preached in *The Great Speckled Bird.*"

Another *Chronicle* native contributor was 1966 Thomas Jefferson High School graduate Joe Schenkman, who drew the cover for the October 15, 1969 issue. "Other than that *Chronicle* cover," he reported, "I went to Pratt in Brooklyn, dropped out to work at the *Rat* underground newspaper, where I met most of the East Coast underground cartoonists." Schenkman then went to San Francisco, where he teamed with many of the West Coast artists and did work for the underground comics *Insect Fear, Gothic Blimp Works* (which started out as a monthly installment to the underground paper the *East Village Other*), *Arcade* and *Short Order Comix* with such artists as Art Speigelman, Bill Griffith, Robert Crumb, Robert Williams and S. Clay Wilson. Back in New York City in the late '70s, Schenkman drew numerous comic features and worked with P.J. O'Rourke as contributing editor of *National Lampoon* magazine.

As an added local bonus, Joe Schenkman's father, Edgar Schenkman, founded the Richmond Symphony in 1957 and served as its music director until 1971.

Like *The Sunflower* a few years earlier, the *Chronicle* paid salespeople to hawk papers on street corners for twenty-five cents per copy (ten cents to the seller, ten cents to the *Chronicle* and five cents to FU), a practice that frequently drew criticism by local business owners and unwanted attention by police.

Bruce Smith told the *Richmond Times Dispatch* in 1969 that there were "some problems" in distributing the paper in Richmond, with police officers ordering street corner vendors to "move on." He said that similar problems were encountered inside Willow Lawn and Southside Plaza shopping centers, when representatives of merchant associations asked the vendors to leave.

Then on August 23, 1969, a young hitchhiker from Florida named Thomas Hubbell was arrested on Atlantic Avenue in Virginia Beach and fined fifty dollars for "selling the *Chronicle* without a license." According to a September 16, 1969 *Times Dispatch* article, Virginia Beach municipal court judge P.B. White fined the "newsboy" fifty dollars—two and a half times the maximum penalty prescribed by the city code, not realizing that the maximum fine was twenty dollars. "The police just used the law to control the hippies," the unapologetic judge told the *Times Dispatch*, "and I went along with them." He went on to say, however, that hippies "must be kept under control" because many of their newspapers are vulgar and obscene. He did admit that the *Chronicle* was neither vulgar nor obscene, "but it had a lot of weird ideas."

Smith said that Hubbell was not a hippie but had "short hair and was clean-shaven" when he was arrested and held on $150 bond. The enterprising young Floridian also sold four more copies of the paper to police officers while in jail.

The Virginia Press Association hired attorney Leon Ely and lodged an official protest of this violation of the state code that noted that "no city, town or county shall require a license for printing or publishing any newspaper." On September 27, several *Chronicle* staffers returned to Virginia Beach and sold papers without incident. Judge White declined to reopen the case on October 8 because Hubbell was a no-show.

One month later, the *Chronicle* reported that a "Mr. Pillow" of Richmond's "totem-pole City Hall" bureaucracy "had his prurient interest aroused by our beautiful page of poems by [*Sunflower* founder] Art Dorow, and consequently, he's trying to pull off an obscenity bust on the *Chronicle*."

Frequent clashes between young fan residents and an overzealous Richmond police force was a frequent topic in the *Chronicle*, especially in the 1100 block of Grove Avenue, where not one but two incidents occurred in 1970 that brought billy club–swinging police and their K9 units. A spontaneous gathering of residents in the street on April 10, 1970, resulted in the police arriving and making two arrests. Word spread that the next night, everyone should come to Grove Avenue, and around 6:00 p.m. on the eleventh, a crowd started forming.

"It's a beautiful scene," claimed an anonymous *Chronicle* writer in the May 1970 issue. "Ask anyone or just listen, and you'll hear them say Wow Man It's Grove Avenue. Wine passing from here to there—the aroma (where is it, where is it), old people, freaks, little kids, straights stopping their cars and joining in…music out of everyone's window flowing through everyone's mind, all united in a beautiful scene of love and brotherhood."

Suddenly, fifty policemen and an "increasing number of growling dogs" showed up, and "so much love turned so bitter in so little time." While the gathering was broken up and ten arrests were made for public drunkenness and disturbing the peace, the disturbance sparked the creation of the Grove Avenue Republic, a loosely based subculture of Grove Avenue residents that attempted to recapture the collective and conciliatory spirit of 1967. "The Grove Avenue republic is people," the *Chronicle* article noted. "People in motion / an identity / communal / peaceful co-existence / an ethnic sub-culture / a fan clique / a subversive organization / the Grove Avenue Republic is YOU."

A later article by Bill Oliver titled "The Impossible Dream…Justice" highlighted both the overreaction of the police and the futility of receiving a fair trial in the Richmond court system after the second Grove Avenue altercation. "Average people, straights, freaks and upper class joes…Beware!!!…if you visit the 'circus court' downtown you DO NOT HAVE A CHANCE."

The FBI had already stated in its COINTELPRO memos its willingness to help make things as difficult as possible for the Richmond hippies. "[A]nother area of potential counterintelligence action is related to the current drive being conducted by the Vice Squad of the Richmond PD concerning a crackdown on drug abuse in the Richmond area, particularly in and around VCU," read a Richmond SAC memo dated April 22, 1969. "As a result of this crackdown by the Vice Squad, SSOC members, as well as anyone who might appear in a hippie-type dress, receive far from a friendly welcome in the Richmond area," adding that at any time "they could be raided on a narcotics charge."

A later statement in that same memo confirmed city officials cooperating with the FBI in their attempts to shut down the SSOC and the Liberated Area shop, including shutting off the utilities and then demanding "higher than normal" deposits and service charges to restore them: "As a tangible result of the above action taken by [redacted] in Richmond, SSOC in Virginia has stated they have had difficulty in organizing and getting any concrete plan of action going in the Richmond metropolitan area due to the fear of arrest and harassment by local authorities."

"The Richmond division recognizes the potential of the New Left and its leaders to inspire activities detrimental to the maintenance of law and order and the crippling of institutions that are necessary to the maintenance of an orderly society."

After November 1969, Katya Sabaroff Taylor's and Bruce Smith's involvement with the *Chronicle* began winding down, and after the dissolution of Free University in March 1970, the paper almost went out of business. Chip Brooks took over as editor after a mass staff exodus, switched from biweekly to a monthly publication schedule and moved the offices first to an apartment on Floyd Avenue and then finally to 1025 West Grace Street, sharing space with the Fan Free Clinic. A classified house ad read simply, "The *Richmond Chronicle* still needs office supplies and equipment, not to mention furniture and money."

"When we got back to Richmond [after the Conference to Combat Fascism]," Smith said, "The student movement we came out of had collapsed. Without a particular purpose, I left the *Chronicle* for Chip and others to develop. Jim Lee and I drifted away from organized politics for a while."

Smith wasn't the only Richmond resident involved in New Left activist movements in other cities. "I went out to Chicago for the second annual riots, got my head busted in and got thrown in jail for thirty days for aggravated battery of a police officer," said Roy Scherer. "They said I beat up three policemen. Understand I used to be a lot bigger than I am now. I came back, and I wrote a firsthand account of it, and it was published in the *Chronicle*. I mailed a copy to my parole officer in Chicago. Never got an answer. Go figure."

"Depressed because I didn't go back to work this eve but stayed home and diddled," Sabaroff Taylor wrote in her last Richmond journal entry dated October 23, 1969. "Anti-climax of returning from the horrible gassing in D.C. in front of the Justice Department—the [*Chronicle*] here seems to be doing OK—Homer [Hurst] and I sold 20 without much effort downtown, but there's a lack of political awareness and I feel cheated and sometimes defeated...Should I leave Richmond soon and get back into rejuvenating circles—LNS, the movement, etc....?"

Sabaroff Taylor left Richmond in February 1970 after serving as editor for almost six months. "I returned to LNS until the spring of 1971, moved to Portland, got involved in the 'women's revolution' which was in full throttle out there. It was then that I changed my name from Nina to Katya and began to study the healing arts."

The *Chronicle* introduced some recurring features in late 1969 and early 1970 in attempts to retain readers and advertisers, including a page of military antiwar news. ("The *Richmond Chronicle* is working with its comrades at Fort Lee and around Amerika [*sic*] to bring the news of the military to the outside world.") A short column titled "Deal" reported the price of illegal drugs on Richmond streets. "Grass is $20. The outlook for grass in March is not very good. Better buy all you can now," one issue noted. "Acid—$5 per tab. When buying acid be sure you know your dealer."

Bruce Smith was correct in his appraisal at the time that the movement was disbanding. By mid-1970, the SSOC had collapsed, and the SDS had broken up into several radical factions, including the Weathermen, who were building bombs and managed to kill three of their own when one accidentally detonated in an apartment in New York City. The revolution was ending as quickly as it had begun; "the '60s" were by then a jumble of fragments including JFK, RFK, MLK, SDS, Weathermen, Beatles, Stonewall, Vietnam, civil rights, Dylan, "Mellow Yello," Country Joe and the Fish and a couple hundred underground papers wondering what the hell just happened.

Editor Chip Brooks, however, seemed unfazed by the declining trend in a June 11, 1970 *Chicago Tribune* news service article titled "Underground Press in U.S. Is Growing." "I expected hostility," the "bearded youth with flowing brown hair" said as he hawked papers in front of an unnamed Richmond shopping center. "But I sold out each issue. Richmond is turning on."

Despite these customer services, and even after teaming in March 1970 with the Charlottesville underground paper the *Virginia Weekly*, offering two-for-one subscriptions, the financial stress was showing in the final three or four issues. It relied more and more on LNS material, local copy was sloppy and headlines were written by hand. Finally, the last issue of the *Richmond Chronicle* was published around early July 1970—almost a year to the day after the debut issue.

Just as the *Chronicle* began winding down, the protest movement in the rest of the United States heated up. In the first week of May, four young people were shot dead by national guardsmen at Ohio's Kent State, and one week later in Washington, D.C., a huge antiwar rally took place. On May 10, 1970, Monroe Park hosted a "Kool-Aid Sunday," featuring live music and information displays set up by Jewish Family Services, Rubicon and the Fan Free Clinic, among others. While the gathering was festive and not at all violent, a seventeen-year-old young man named Wilmer Donovan Jr. was killed when the tiered cast-iron fountain he and a friend had climbed on suddenly snapped and crushed him in the surrounding wading pool. Stark photos of the accident, taken by James Woodard III, appeared on the front page of the *Times Dispatch*.

"At present, there are no known New Left organized groups active within the Richmond division," noted an FBI COINTELPRO memo dated October 6, 1970.

Phase One, 1970–71

In September 1970, after the *Chronicle* folded, Dale Milford, Bill Oliver, Ben Smith and several former *Chronicle* artists, writers and photographers started a monthly publication called *Phase One* as a Fan-based successor to the *Chronicle*, with a stronger emphasis on investigative reporting "about issues the traditional media was unwilling to pursue," according to Oliver. The subhead over the logo read "Journal of Revolutionary Times."

"I don't remember the total number of issues, but it did become a legitimate news business when the [Richmond] Department of Public Safety issued press credentials to the staff—of course, everyone had to get finger printed!" Oliver said in 2013. "Dale [Milford] was associated with Squeezo Graphics and was doing art and lights while side-lining with *Phase One*. Like him, I had several jobs in the Fan and did things with *Phase One* when I could. It was not a financial success, so we all moved on into other areas."

A self-proclaimed member of the Liberation News Service (although not listed in LNS archives), *Phase One* was headquartered at 1033 West Grace Street and focused on Fan and certain national events of interest to former *Chronicle* readers, including news of the inevitable drug busts and the D.C. antiwar rally.

Phase One described firsthand a second confrontation with police occurring on October 12, 1970, following a reading by Beat poet Allen Ginsburg to an overflow crowd at the VCU old gym. At the end of the reading, Ginsburg—who was paid about $200 to come—was handed a flyer, and he announced there was going to be a block party (once again) in the 1100 block of Grove Avenue. At about 10:00 p.m., a band started playing on a second-floor balcony, free beer started flowing and soon more than 1,200 people were milling in the street. The trouble started when a K9 unit policeman stopped by and let his unleashed dog out of the car. Soon more police came with their dogs, and for more than an hour, they worked to break up the party while being pelted with bottles, rocks and bricks. One policeman was knocked unconscious by a brick thrown from a roof at the corner of Grove and Lombardy. Two cruisers were spray-painted with the words "Pig," "Anarchy" and "Oink." Four VCU students were bitten by police dogs, two policemen were injured and about seventeen were arrested. In an attempt to quell the violence, Ginsburg reportedly assisted in persuading about three hundred revelers to go to Monroe Park, with the understanding that those arrested would be released—only either that was

Phase One, December 1970. Art by Phil Trumbo. *Courtesy Steve Wall.*

a rumor or the police reneged, and many of those people, chanting "free the people," went back to Grove Avenue.

"What an evening!" recalled Steve Wall. "When the police came down Grove, the people scattered. I looked around, and there were about thirty people in my eight-by-ten room on the third floor."

Phase One's account of that riot was written by Artist Dale Milford in volume 1, number 3: "Violence and bloodshed have become a part of our lives…The Grove Avenue incident proved this to be true in police as well as young people. Few of these people wanted violence, but because they acted in haste, in fear, they received it…At this time things are tragic because all we know is violence…right wing violence instigated by Nixon, left wing violence by revolutionaries…we are committing national suicide and very few realize that the way through salvation is through peace, understanding and social action, not through reprisal, restriction and revenge."

A year after both the original *Chronicle* and *Phase One* folded, Chip Brooks tried to recapture that outlaw spirit and "turn Richmond on" again by rebooting the *Chronicle* as a weekly broadsheet newspaper. He retained the name and some of the original staff, like Dale Milford and John Gilmore Jr., and added several new faces.

Now located at 1205 West Main Street, the July 16, 1971 issue of the new *Richmond Chronicle* was less radical in its appearance and content than its recently retired tabloid predecessor. It featured more essays than news stories pertinent to leftist social causes but retained little of its former underground editorial fire. Almost all of the articles were reprinted from the Copley News Service, with a scarce few local stories on local events running with no bylines.

Content varied widely, from a cover story on America's pending police state reprinted from the *Nation* to an article on Virginia drug paraphernalia laws. There was a column on organic gardening, record reviews by WGOE radio program director Ken Booton, a horoscope, a crossword puzzle and syndicated comics by non-Richmond artists. The issue concluded on page 14 with a ten-thousand-word manifesto entitled "Thou Shalt Not Kill" from an anonymous Richmond conscientious objector.

As shown by this *Chronicle*, the New Left underground movement in Richmond was on its last legs. There were no subsequent issues of the *Richmond Chronicle* or *Phase One*, closing that chapter for good.

"I never remember going out to an expensive restaurant, or even a movie, but rather throwing myself into the work of the day, which was heady," Katya Sabaroff Taylor wrote of her time in Richmond with the *Chronicle*. "I loved my little apartment in the Fan District where we paid 75

Richmond Chronicle, "rebooted," July 16, 1971. *Courtesy the author.*

dollars a month including utilities. We were poor but very happy. Just throwing my lot in with the movement to make a difference was the best entertainment there was, and I am proud of what we did, then, and the result of our labors, now."

THE *COMMONWEALTH TIMES*, 1969–PRESENT

VCU is a curiosity, a factory for turning out professionals, but it has not fully enjoyed the love of taxpayers, many of whom tend to see all university students as a collection of free-love, pot-smoking bums.
—Howard Ozmon, quoted in the 1973 VCU Cobblestone *yearbook*

It's not for knowledge that we come to college but to work for the Commonwealth Times.
—wall graffiti at the Commonwealth Times *offices, 1978*

On July 1, 1968, Richmond Professional Institute and the downtown Medical College of Virginia merged and officially become Virginia Commonwealth University, and to reflect the change, the RPI school newspaper, the *Proscript*, became the *Commonwealth Times* (*CT*).

The September 10, 1969 "Special Orientation Issue" of the *CT*, under the coeditorship of Christy Cook and Jean Talley, stated that the name change was done "so that unity may be enhanced between the two divisions of VCU." "This issue marks the beginning of a new phase in student journalism," a far-sighted editorial noted. "The electronic media is taking over—even on this campus. The printed word has been delegated to a back seat. By using creative techniques and originality, we hope to make a place in front for the *Commonwealth Times*."

Like its predecessor, the *Proscript*, the *CT* functioned as a typical and very conservative college news organ for the first few years, describing ring

Commonwealth Times,
November 14, 1978.
Courtesy the author.

dances, fraternity activities, collegiate and intramural sports and other generic college-related information.

A break in the staid conservatism was provided by local poet and (twenty-nine-year-old) VCU sophomore Rik Davis with a humor column called "Electric Kumquat Cabala" that debuted in the October 15, 1969 issue. According to Davis—a familiar persona around VCU and the Fan in his safari hat and pipe—the title evolved "because everything is electric these days. Kumquat, because it adds class and visual imagery and because kumquats make you horny. And because Cabala means a secret, encoded attitude toward the ultimate confrontation with life."

In March 1971, under Editor-in-Chief Ellen Hawthorne, the *CT* ran the first article on the recently formed Gay Liberation Front, formed by VCU alumnus Kenneth Pederson to raise gay awareness in Richmond and VCU, with the headquarters in the somewhat notorious 1100 block of Grove

Avenue (home of the Grove Avenue Republic a year earlier). "The following article is being printed in the *Times* in order to help explain and clarify what the movement is all about and is not intended either to support or condemn Gay Liberation," read a somewhat nervous editor's note.

"Gay liberation can't be ignored because it is here," stated writers Gary Thompson and Mike Whitlow. "Gay people want to destroy the popular conception that homosexuals are ill, 'sick people.' Heterosexual society's psychiatrists can't cure homosexuals, but can only help them learn to live with homosexuality. They tell you to go ahead and be homosexual 'in your closet,' but not to let on that you are in public." Whether this story was met with anger, support or indifference, subsequent issues of the *CT* contained not one letter or response to it.

In the fall of 1971, the *Commonwealth Times* split from the jurisdiction of the VCU journalism department and began publishing on an independent basis. Editor Bill Royall said at the time that the divorce between the paper and the journalism department was precipitated when the department found it "could not fulfill its academic obligations and concurrently run the student newspaper."

Professor Bill Turpin said in a 1971 *Richmond Chronicle* story that the break was amicable and in line with what was happening to other student newspapers across the country. "Students don't want the kind of dictatorial, overseeing control which has characterized institutions in the past," Turpin said. "They don't want someone to tell them what their moral codes should be. They are too sophisticated for that."

The *CT* was then officially autonomous, breaking from its role as a corporate organ and starting a trajectory as a more alternative community medium. But since the paper was partially supported by student activity fees, it was still overseen by a newly created VCU Media Board, presided over by journalism professor George Crutchfield, that had no say in the day-to-day newspaper operations, which that semester was headed by Editor Mariane Matera.

"The semester I was editor, I was also profoundly pregnant," Matera said in 2013. "In fact, the night before I gave birth in May 1971, I built my last *Commonwealth Times* and carried the box to the printer downtown. I thought I wet the bed, but it was my water breaking the next morning, and by that evening, I was a mother."

In September 1972, the *CT* switched to a broadsheet layout that intentionally made it more resemble the *Richmond Times Dispatch* than a college tabloid and then elected art history major Edwin Slipek Jr. as executive editor the next year.

"I went to lunch with Bill Royall at the old Angelo's Hot Dogs on 4ᵗʰ Street because he liked one article I wrote on the new business building," recalled Slipek in a 2013 interview. "He said, 'You're going to be the editor next year,' and I said, 'Well I think there are a lot of journalism majors standing in line for that job,' but it was an elected position. It was a major upset for a student from the school of the arts to become executive editor over folks who had been paying their dues for many, many years."

"I was interested in making the paper more magazine-like and more feature-like," Slipek continued, "but again my staff was from journalism, which I wasn't, so we stayed broadsheet."

After Slipek left in May 1972, the paper switched back to the familiar tabloid size, drawing comparisons to another newly published Richmond tabloid, the *Richmond Mercury*. Two years later, under Steve Lasko, the *CT* suddenly found itself about $11,000 in debt. "Without Steve Lasko, the paper could have gone under," claimed an editorial in the May 2, 1974 issue. "He spent countless hours trying to straighten out one terrific mess. And straighten it out he did."

After Lasko's tenure, a succession of editors continued pulling the newsmagazine further back from the traditional formats into a bold new direction as a somewhat independent weekly. Under Brett Averill, the paper was broken into more distinct sections, titled Opinion, News, Folio (Arts and Culture), Sports, Calendar and Classifieds and, for the first time, abandoned the more traditional "wall of type" cover to instead devote the entire cover to an illustration and title blurb, making the magazine more *Rolling Stone* than *Times Dispatch*.

"I learned a lot in that job. The *CT* had the latest Compugraphic and a Verityper for headlines, and a waxer and the whole nine yards," wrote Bill Kovarik, who now teaches journalism at Radford University. "The newsroom was a lot of fun and, like all newsrooms, a humming center of our community. You met everyone, some you liked, some you didn't and some who just left you flat-footed and amazed at the human condition—like Dennis Dyke, [a man] who was elected prom queen one year, who came flouncing through every now and then. Or the VCU police chief who was caught with tens of thousands of rounds of automatic weapons ammo in his car, and of course, everyone wondered what the hell he was going to do with it all."

"I was there at the beginning of 1975," said Waynesboro musician and music teacher Rebby Sharp. "The whole time there was head-butting between the staff and the department. It was a time when the *Mercury* had just stopped, and the staff of the *CT* thought that it could be a neighborhood paper."

"One of the big issues of the community at that time was VCU's expansion into Oregon Hill," Sharp explained. "So the *CT* was a mouthpiece for that conflict. There was a drive year after year with the master plan to convert it into having a campus because of the way the state allocated the money. Did they ever go west? Onto West Ave? No, they went north, and south into Oregon Hill, which was being sectioned off and stripped apart year by year, and VCU was just a part of that."

Originally located on the top floor of the VCU Administration Building at 901 West Franklin before moving to a carriage house on Shafter Street in 1972, the *CT* offices moved again in 1975 to 916 West Franklin Street. There, two Douglas Freeman High School buddies accelerated the magazine even faster into this more community-oriented graphic and editorial direction. Under the leadership of Peter Blake (son of VCU history professor Dr. William Blake) in 1977, the *CT* embraced a bold graphic style and a strong sense of humor, thanks to the presence also of Peter's friend Bill Pahnelas, art director Rob Sauder-Conrad, photographer Tim Wright and a similar-thinking group of artists, editors and writers.

"Working at the *CT* was the best job I ever have had," said Peter Blake in 2012. "I worked side by side with some of the smartest and most provocative people I have ever known. We came from places like Buffalo Gap, Fort Defiance, Berryville, Damascus, Victoria and Stuart's Draft. Still, we managed to find a common voice that spoke to the VCU community."

"The *CT* offices those years had a certain atmosphere of animal excitement," recalled Sauder-Conrad on his experiences at the paper from 1977 to 1979. "Music was constant; Ramones, Sex Pistols, what have you. And at the drop of a hat, we felt free to throw our old, beat-up wooden chairs up and down our old, beat-up second-floor hallway. It didn't feel like anything was being destroyed; it felt like something was being liberated."

The year 1978 was a culturally rich one for the Richmond and VCU communities. Pop artist Andy Warhol breezed into town in January for an opening of his work at the Virginia Museum of Fine Arts on Boulevard. "During the actual question-answer period, I had to feel a little for Andy Warhol," wrote *CT* reporter Michael Sherbert for the January 24, 1978 issue. "His strange white hair and frightened eyes made him look like a hunted rabbit or a Barbie doll that had the shit beat out of it."

Commonwealth Times, January 31, 1978. Art by Michael Sherbert. *Courtesy VCU Cabell Library Special Collections, Richmond, Virginia.*

Timothy Leary came to the Mosque on March 30 to attempt to explain his theory SMILE (Space Migration, Intelligence Increase and Life Extension). As he spoke, he was shaken by an anonymous Richmonder who bypassed security, ran out on stage and hurled a cream pie in his face. Leary crossed his legs, laughed nervously and continued his talk. "My friends, you are not terrestrials," he rambled, wiping cream from his eyes. "Prepare to unbuckle your seat belts and leave the planet earth. There's

Commonwealth Times, October 31, 1978. Art by the Ramones. *Courtesy the author.*

no reason why anyone in this room need ever die. At the present time, medical science, physiology, genetics, bio-chemistry amino acid magicians are at the threshold of discovering how the RNA tape loop create aging and death."

"I thought he was a galloping bore," VCU painting professor Jewett Campbell told his class the next day.

The Ramones came to town for the VCU Halloween Dance and graciously sprawled on the floor to draw the cover of the October 31, 1978 issue. Dr. Hunter S. Thompson also came to the Mosque in a forty-one-foot Winnebago motor home, and the *CT* ran a transcription of his entire addled Q&A in front of the Mosque audience.

"Working at the *CT* was so much more than buying Black Label beer at 6 a.m., when the 7-Eleven opened, or sleeping in a closet because if we went home we would not have time to drive to the printer in the morning," wrote

Blake in 2012. "It was more than talking an angry reporter off the ledge for the way we edited her article, or trying to soothe an artist after we put her drawing on page six instead of on the cover."

Not only was the slowly expanding urban VCU conducive to the countercultural, even antisocial behavior of the staffers, but the building housing the *CT* offices was also a perfect melting pot for the eccentricity inside. A William Poindexter–designed Moorish turreted brownstone built in 1891, the Millhiser House at 916 West Franklin Street contained such oddities as a revolving bookcase in the master study downstairs where supposedly owner and businessman Gustavus Millhiser could beat a hasty exit if he saw an unwanted visitor coming up the front steps. Cast-iron "firebacks" in the numerous fireplaces adorned with witches, cauldrons and other Shakespeare- and mythology-inspired scenes added to the sense of offbeat mystery that pervaded the labyrinthine three-story building.

With the election of a bearded and crazy-haired English major named Bill Pahnelas to executive editor and the hiring of art director Sue Dayton in September 1979, the paper exploded into a graphic *enfant terrible* of the Richmond print scene, breaking completely from boilerplate college-based news reporting and encouraging commentaries, news analysis and more artistic contributions that cut even further away from the VCU campus and explored Richmond's sometimes sleazy underbelly. Dayton's frequently eccentric page layouts coupled with Pahnelas's musings on the seedier side of Grace Street and all-night drugstore lunch counters sprinkled among the more classic college reporting frequently left readers (and many fellow staff members) scratching their heads—to the consternation of those VCU journalism and commercial art professors who handed over their influence almost a decade earlier.

"[We] caught hell for combining what we thought was fine art with graphic art. Early punk, that's what it was," said Sue Dayton in 2013. "The [Commercial Art] department gave us so much shit for experimenting with covers and inside design. And after [production] was all done, we were among the other transients who ordered the ninety-nine-cent breakfast at People's Drugstore, looking into the mirror behind the counter and writing poetry."

That "early punk" style started a trend of outspoken unhappiness with the paper. "Last week's 'Skinnerview,' with its display of underwater photography and a full page dedicated to dog shit are consistent expressions of the *CT*'s scatological approach to reality by which journalism at VCU has sunk to a new low," wrote Carlos Potes. "Perhaps sometime in the future we will be treated to a scratch 'n' sniff issue."

A few issues later, the paper began to temper the design standards while better reflecting its urban locale and drawing heavily on the tremendous talent pool available within the university student body and faculty to create some truly original and sometimes controversial work. Under the tutelage of this particular group of editors and managers (who all sported GPAs in the 3.75–4.0 range), the *Commonwealth Times* burst to creative life and swept award after award at local and national levels, including a coveted "Superior" award for graphic layout at the National Collegiate Press Association (NCPA) convention in New York City in 1980.

"This is what all of you should be doing!" said a judge at the final awards ceremony in the conference room at the former Doral Inn, holding up to the entire convention assembly the *CT* summer 1980 issue, whose cover was nothing but a television test pattern and a logo. "You should be having fun, breaking the rules, because this is the only chance in your life you'll have to do it!"

Actively heeding the advice of the judge, the *CT* staff returned to Richmond with business major Michael S. Fuller at the editorial helm and focused on journalistic, editorial and business, as well as graphic innovation.

"Mike Fuller changed the *CT*," said Rebby Sharp of Fuller's introduction to the paper in 1975 as an ad rep. "Mike was so square, but he was so smart, and he was the most organized, the least counterculture and was going to sell ads and make the *CT* independently viable. People were skeptical because he was a business guy when we didn't know any business people."

Encouraged by businessman Fuller's "square" but liberal leadership, the *CT* continued breaking controversial stories that sometimes rubbed the campus raw, raising concerns of its portrayal of the campus image. An obscenity-soaked exposé of a local teenage, drug-addled, boy-pimp musician who went by the name Dickie Disgusting appeared in the September 23, 1980 issue. A photo of a "glory hole" in the Business Building men's restrooms appeared with an accompanying story of the numerous arrests for solicitations. Finally, the *CT* continued a tradition of publishing a list of the salaries of every single VCU employee, obtained through Freedom of Information. Features like these sent many faculty (whose salaries were now public knowledge) and student government types into a tailspin, moving some of them to petition that "out of control" publication that in their opinion more closely resembled the *Weekly World News* than a college newsmagazine.

Commonwealth Times, summer 1980. Design by Ron Thomas Smith. *Courtesy the author.*

"It hits the fringe…does not hit the center of VCU," said Dr. Al Matthews, then dean of student life. "It's almost a cheap shot at sensationalism."

A former student reported that a certain political science professor put the salary list in a different perspective, telling one of his classes that he didn't really mind everyone seeing how pathetic his salary was.

While most students sincerely enjoyed the paper's sometimes offbeat editorial policy and scintillating graphics, as evidenced by a press run that had to be increased from ten thousand to twelve thousand weekly copies to accommodate demand, there was a very vocal minority that called for it to either be shut down or handed back over to the mass communications department. One journalism major who chose to remain unidentified in a December 7, 1980 *Richmond Times Dispatch* article about the paper headlined "Commonwealth Times: Good News, Bad News" referred to the *CT* staff as "a defensive little group of kids that think they have this wonderful mandate from the students for existing." The anonymous student pouted, saying, "That is not the forum I want for my writing."

But more eyebrows were raised by VCU president Dr. Edmund Ackell in that same interview when he claimed that "[t]his kind of article [the Dickie Disgusting interview] does a great disservice to our institution, and raises a serious question in my mind about the appropriateness of the *Times* as it is presently identified with this university."

Perceiving Dr. Ackell's statement as a threat, former editor Peter Blake responded to the fan-blown excrement with an opinion in the *CT* signed by all twenty-one staff members calling for recognition of "[t]he diverse and sometimes unpleasant cosmos of VCU…In short, something is wrong when a single interview we print in which 'bad words' (or worse—a bad attitude) leads people to suggest that the *Times* is unreal, and is creating an inaccurate vision of VCU."

"VCU is a different kind of institution," noted an equally diplomatic George Crutchfield in the same *Times Dispatch* story. "It's just grown all of a sudden and become a big, major university. That changes the role of the student newspaper a little."

Fortunately, cooler heads prevailed at 8:00 a.m. Funding Committee hearings. The motion to defund died, and an uneasy truce began between the magazine, student government and President Ackell—at least until 1983, when Dr. Ackell cut the *CT* off from further interviews after Editor Ronnie Greene questioned his presence on the board of directors of the Whittaker Corporation, a California-based firm that sold $1 million worth of medical supplies annually to the university's own medical campus, constituting a possible conflict of interest. In 1985, the cone of silence was lifted.

"Leonardo Live at the Vatican." Art by Ronnie Sampson for the *Commonwealth Times*, summer 1980. *Courtesy the author.*

"Sure, we screwed up famously, but we also came together in imaginative and creative ways," said Peter Blake.

Editorial controversy aside, the weekly magazine flourished creatively. Heavily influenced by New York– and San Francisco–based publications like *Village Voice*, *Wet* and *Boulevards*, no creative stone went unturned, and even nonstudent artists, graduate students and fine arts instructors came to the paper brandishing portfolios and asking for illustration assignments.

"I was taking some classes with [VCU art instructor] Mallory Callan, and he was encouraging me to get some printed pieces and get that experience,"

Artist Kelly Alder said in 2013. "I always wanted to be a commercial artist, and [the *CT*] seemed like a good place to start." A spectacular artist, Alder had a cover assignment within a week, and he remained a fixture at the *CT* for two years before continuing to earn a living for years as one of Richmond's most sought-after illustrators.

The *CT* office from the mid-1970s into 1982 was a work of radical art; graffiti and murals drawn directly on the hallowed plaster of the Millhiser House displayed complex felt-tip cityscape murals, cartoons and such zingers as "Who killed Bambi?" "No future," "I'm a sexual intellectual" (a polite way of calling themselves a "fucking know-it-all") and "It's not for knowledge that I come to college but to work at the *Commonwealth Times*," among others. VCU Evening College president John Mapp gladly submitted to having his picture taken signing his name on the production room wall just after Student Activities director Ken Ender told the staff to stop writing on the walls.

As Dr. Crutchfield noted, VCU suddenly grew up as an urban institution during the 1970s into the 1980s, and a similar raw, explosive attitude that spawned Richmond's amazing punk rock and new wave music movement dominated both the art school and the *CT*. The staff simply wanted the magazine to reflect that more boldly artistic and diversified market, as well as exploit the talents of the various schools—and, like the judge said, have fun and break the rules.

The offices also became a hangout for a sundry mixture of Richmond creators, characters and even crazies. Poet and novelist John Alspaugh recruited Bill Pahnelas and Dale Brumfield to typeset and design his first collection of poetry, titled *Everything Dark Is a Doorway* (Palimpsest, 1982). A local (male) punk rocker showed up one Friday night in a woman's party dress and intentionally sliced his own bicep numerous times with an X-Acto knife, dripping blood on one of the page layouts. One disturbed young man who was convinced that his brain was controlled by a computer in the VCU School of Business popped in periodically to brag that it was his best friend who threw a pie in the face of counterculture guru Timothy Leary during that live appearance at the Mosque in 1979. Filmmaker John Waters got a kick out of the office walls when he came for an interview during the Richmond premiere of his 1982 movie, *Polyester*.

By 1983, the troublemaking and hard-living old-timers had graduated from their positions of authority and had to be dragged out into the working world, while more level-headed current staffers and a new group of young students that had rotated in wanted to retain at least a touch

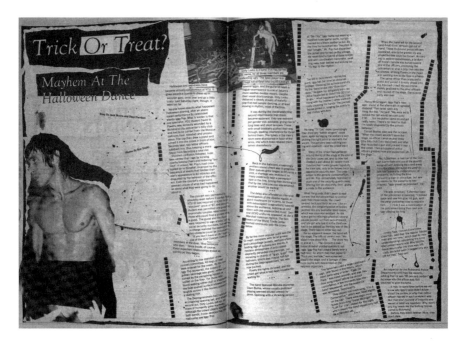

Iggy Pop riot at the Mosque centerspread, *Commonwealth Times*, November 1, 1981. Story by Jack Moore and Dave Harrison. Photos by Ron Smith. Design by Ronnie Sampson and Dale Brumfield. *Courtesy VCU Cabell Library Special Collections, Richmond, Virginia.*

of the eccentricity but at the same time were eager to develop more seriousness to the news reporting and production process. The leadership throughout the late 1980s of people like R. Steven Landes (as of 2013, the Twenty-fifth District delegate in the Virginia House of Representatives), Janet Moore, Gary Levine, Pam Kiely, Rich Radford and Ronnie Greene tempered the magazine's broadsided counterculturalism and frequent middle finger to the administration and student government to take a more graphically straightforward approach, choosing to appeal as a magazine more editorially directed to the VCU student body than to the surrounding community.

Still, the wackiness was slow leaving. Steve Landes came back to his office after a weekend off in 1982 and found that it had been wrapped with seeming miles of IBM Selectrix typewriter ribbon, finished off with nail polish–painted cooked hot dogs dangling from the ceiling.

"The *Commonwealth Times* was a hangout, not just a working environment," said Don Harrison, who served as arts editor from 1983 to 1986, echoing a sentiment of almost everyone who worked there since its inception. "It was a great place to be, but there was frequently a lot of yelling and drama due to people bringing their personal problems to the paper."

One example of drama was when a managing editor and the sports editor, after an evening of drinking and bragging, became concerned that some VCU athletes were not academically eligible for their respective sports, so they admitted to misrepresenting themselves and entered an athletic department office and photocopied student athlete transcripts. Fortunately, the next morning, they claimed to have sobered up and destroyed the copies. Still, the managing editor was forced to resign, and the *CT* endured accusations of a coverup, spurred by a letter to the editor written by former contributor Ned Scott Jr. "The paper's behavior during this episode has been appalling," wrote Peter MacPherson in a *mea culpa* in the January 23, 1984 issue. "The *Times* is quick to jump on everyone else when they're screwing up but not quite so quick to turn the spotlight inward when the situation dictates."

While the paper still drew on the talents of the art school, Harrison reiterated that there was a tug of war in the 1980s between the editorial side of the paper and the artistic side: "I was blasted once at a staff meeting by almost everybody, who said the arts features were becoming too weird. We were doing pieces about trips through music store cut-out bins and spending the night at a crisis hot line. We had a skydiving story. They said, 'You should be doing more about campus,' but I thought the pressure was off to worry so much about the campus—the news section covered the campus really well [under] Ronnie Green and Rich Radford, who were muckrakers in the best possible way."

Coverage periodically strayed off campus. For the November 1985 issue, photographer Michael Cope turned in show-stopping pictures of a little-known band called the Red Hot Chili Peppers playing at a local club. Then, in a nod to their recent counterculture history, a 1987 issue ran a punkish centerspread feature on local shock bands GWAR and Death Piggy, followed by a notice on the very next page that former Nixon hatchetman G. Gordon Liddy was going to be speaking at the Commons Theater.

The magazine also maintained its strong sense of humor, courtesy of Don Harrison and Dave Harrison (no relation), aided by the adaptations of boring press releases and the sometimes last-minute inclusions of creative "house ads" to fill gaps in the layout caused either by a cancelled advertisement or a photo that never showed up. "Kurt Vonnegut fans can meet their hero as he signs one of his books if they care to fly to Dallas," claimed an arts short under the heading "Folio Notes" in a March 1986 issue. "You'd know about things like this too, if you read half the press handouts we do."

Don Harrison went on to publish the Hampton, Virginia–based alternative monthlies *Catharsis* from 1989 to 1993 and *Grip* from 1996 to 1999, both of which were distributed in Richmond and in other Virginia localities.

In 1989, at the close of the "decade of fear" (as described by a handful of *CT* staffers a decade earlier), the magazine came full circle and settled back in a comfortable position once again as a college news delivery vehicle, not as (some would describe) an axe-grinding pseudo-underground mouthpiece for "a defensive little group of kids." While the students were not necessarily changing, VCU definitely was, with massive construction projects spreading out tentacle-like from its former home base of Franklin and Shafer Streets north and west over and beyond Broad Street and east past Belvidere Street. President Eugene Trani adopted a more bottom line–oriented approach to university affairs, and the *Commonwealth Times* seemed to adapt that buttoned-down style to the news and to its presentation, again reflecting the environment in which it is produced—a high-tech, graffiti-free office in West Broad Street's Media Center.

"I was interested in something else," Rob Sauder-Conrad said recently about his tenure there in the mid-1970s, "although I'm not sure I can articulate exactly what, even today. Something about freedom and throwing chairs and loud music. What good fortune for me that I found a pod of weird-smart-funny kids and was accepted within. Such a good thing!"

In 2013, the *CT* celebrates its forty-fourth birthday.

THE *RICHMOND MERCURY,*
1972–1975

The Mercury *was a lot of things but mostly it was a state of mind. We
had strong goals, a clear target and a wonderful antagonist in the complacent
Richmond dailies. We had a great town to work in, with larger-than-life
personalities and a façade of gentility and political etiquette covering an
underworld of cut-throat, back-room politics and race hatred.*
–former Richmond Mercury *reporter Glenn Frankel, quoted in*
Style Weekly, *January 10, 1989*

*They did some excellent work and some that was not good at all. Like all
publications, they were uneven.*
–Richmond Times Dispatch *managing editor Alf Goodykoontz on the
folding of the* Richmond Mercury *in the August 19, 1975*
Fredericksburg Free Lance-Star

Around April 1972, a couple of well-dressed guys walked into a brand-new repertory movie house on Grace Street called the Biograph wanting
to know if manager Terry Rea would be interested in purchasing ad space
in their tabloid newspaper that was going to start publishing in September.
"They came by with that prototype issue and an ad packet months before
the first issue," Rea recalled. "I think we saw each other as proof that the
world was becoming a better place."

That "prototype" was volume 0, number 0 of the *Richmond Mercury*, named
after H.L. Mencken's humor and commentary magazine the *American Mercury*

and the next tabloid newsmagazine to publish in Richmond since the July 1971 dissolution of the last alternative publication, the *Richmond Chronicle*.

The *Mercury* was temperamentally miles apart from the *Chronicle* and unique in its approach to news coverage. While the *Chronicle*, with its dedicated volunteer army of social militants, radicals and VCU art students, angrily bulldozed its way through Richmond, the *Mercury* instead rolled into town armed with impeccable credentials wrapped in Harvard and UVA blazers, looking not to replace the mainstream media but to fearlessly augment it with "no pandering" and a "more adventuresome kind of real in-depth, investigative reporting," according to cofounder and staff writer Garrett Epps in the September 13, 1972 *Richmond Times Dispatch*.

Epps, Rob Buford IV and Edmund Rennolds III established the *Richmond Mercury* believing that the city was ready for a new alternative news source that grew out of their desire to come back and start an improvement process, not follow the status quo. "After our collegiate years, we were left with a shared belief that Richmond was a good place to live and the common hope that we might keep it that way, perhaps make it a little better," noted the "Letter from the Editors" in the prototype issue. "Richmond in the early 1970s—like the rest of America—still faces a struggle for social and economic justice. A drive from the spacious houses on the James to the crumbling shacks of Oregon Hill is all the convincing needed. The split between the races needs to be healed and Richmond's large Black population must be given the opportunities in education, business and society that have been denied to them for so long."

"Garrett and I had a couple of meetings, and he was picking my brain about things he ought to know about life in a university town, his hometown," said Edwin Slipek Jr. "He asked me as editor of the *Commonwealth Times* if I would do an article about VCU's impact on the Fan District and in the immediate area. Then when I left the *CT*, I went to the *Mercury* as a freelance art and architecture writer."

It wasn't just the love of and a desire to unite the city that led to the creation of the *Mercury*; the presence of the two Richmond daily papers and the virulent segregationist reputation they had championed on their editorial pages prompted the founders into action as well. Epps confirmed that many young journalists at that time did not see working for Richmond newspapers as an ethical option because of their segregationist reputation and hard right-wing stance.

"That's the thing about Richmond at the time, from a young person's perspective," said former *Mercury* writer Bill Kovarik. "It was a highly

The Sunflower, November 16, 1967. Artist unknown. *Courtesy VCU Cabell Library Special Collections, Richmond, Virginia.*

Richmond Chronicle, May 1, 1970. *Courtesy VCU Cabell Library Special Collections, Richmond, Virginia.*

Richmond Chronicle, October 15, 1969. Art by Joe Schenkman. *Courtesy Special Collections, University of Virginia Library, Charlottesville, Virginia.*

Above, left:
ThroTTle,
April 1983.
Art by Doug
Dobey. *Courtesy
the author.*

Above, right:
ThroTTle,
April 1984.
Art by Joseph
Seipel. *Courtesy
the author.*

Bottom:
ThroTTle,
March
1985. Art by
Don (Bone)
Schrader.
*Courtesy the
author.*

ThroTTle, November 1983.
Art by Bill Nelson. *Courtesy
the author.*

ThroTTle,
February 1984.
Art by Dale
Brumfield.
Courtesy the author.

ThroTTle, September 1984. Art by Anne Peet. *Courtesy the author.*

Hardball, volume 1, number 1, October 1982. Various artists. Design by Michael Clautice. *Courtesy Peter Blake.*

Clue, November
1984. Philip Johnson
portrait by Robert
Meganck. *Courtesy
Edwin Slipek Jr.*

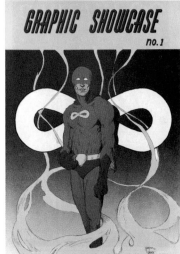

Graphic Showcase, volume 1, number 1, 1967.
Art by Michael Kaluta. *Courtesy VCU Cabell
Library Special Collections, Richmond, Virginia.*

Graphic Showcase, number 3, 1970. Art by Gray Morrow. *Courtesy VCU Cabell Library Special Collections, Richmond, Virginia.*

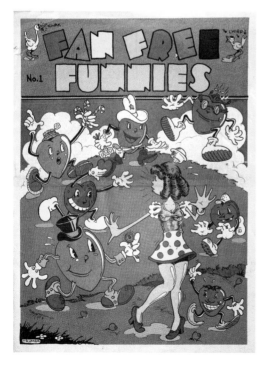

Fan Free Funnies, number 1, February 1973. Art by Phil Trumbo. *Courtesy VCU Cabell Library Special Collections, Richmond, Virginia.*

Boys and Girls Grow Up, number 5, 1985. Art by Amy Crehore. *Courtesy Tom Campagnoli.*

Scratchez, number 8, 1986. Art by Jeff Gaither. *Courtesy the author.*

Twenty-five cents

the richmond mercury

April 11, 1972   Volume 0, Number 0   Richmond, Virginia

Inside:

THE COMING OF THE CABLE. Richmond firms bid for the lucrative franchise. Page 3.
BUSING AND THE CONSTITUTION. The politicans are monkeying with a legal buzz saw—a Mercury point of view. Page 6.
ITT IS STILL IN TROUBLE. Jack Anderson's not letting up on his favorite corporate giant. Read his column on page 7.
MYTHS AND CADILLACS. A look at the writer behind The Last Picture Show. Page 8.
THE GODFATHER. A fine film with a uniquely American story to tell. Page 9.

Unfreezing the watermelon

Can Howell deliver for the little guy?

by Charles Hite

The administrative and legal aide to Virginia's Lieutenant Governor bursts through the door into the bustling staff offices and without breaking his stride offers profuse apologies for being forty minutes late. He performs the cordial greeting and handshake of long separation as if he really means them, then sits down at his desk, leans back in his chair and explains that he has just lost all sense of time while rummaging about the voluminous files of the State Corporation Commission.

Shaking his head, he pulls a packet out of his notebook: *You really have to watch these guys. Keep tabs on them. Look at this. Just look. No one was informed they were going to do this.*

A letter. An order from the State Corporation Commission allowing the C&P Telephone Company to keep the $4½ million it had been ordered to repay its customers until its appeal to the Supreme Court of Virginia goes through.

I just object to the fact that no one bothered to tell anyone about this. It's typical of the way the SCC operates.

Another packet plops on the desk, an intervention filed with the SCC against Vepco's proposed $79 million rate hike, the largest ever asked. These are real big boys: Allied Chemical, Anheuser Busch,

continued on page four

Richmond Mercury, prototype issue, April 1972. Art by David Ritchie. *Courtesy VCU Cabell Library Special Collections, Richmond, Virginia.*

stratified society. There was the aristocracy, and there was everyone else. The aristocracy got away with all kinds of criminal activity, but the law enforcement system preyed on the weak, the hippies, the African Americans."

"The *Mercury* was launched by twenty-two-year-old kids just out of college who were utterly clueless about magazine publishing," said former editor Gene Ely II. "But that startup crew was wonderful. They were smart, they wrote like the wind, they were fearless and they were totally likeable as people."

While the *Mercury* was definitely irreverent, alternative and leftist politically, there was nothing traditionally "underground" about it. It broke ranks with both of Richmond's previous two alternative papers by utilizing investors, including Best Products Company president Sydney Lewis and publisher Edmond Rennolds III. It had a solid business plan, a marketing survey that showed the environment was conducive to a news tabloid and a paid staff.

"The problem back then was that there were no business models to follow," said Ely. "It was all new, uncharted territory. So-called alternative papers existed in just a few American cities, and none in cities the size of Richmond."

Part of their plan according to Buford was their willingness "to offend people" to get the story. "We call it 'outsider journalism,'" he told the *Times Dispatch*. "That means we don't have to go on the dole to get the news."

While the initial financial situation was, according to Rennolds, "secure but volatile," he claimed to have "informal commitments" for the $150,000 needed to launch the *Mercury*, saying also that the paper would need a circulation of at least ten to fifteen thousand per week to survive, based on advertising revenues and the selling price.

The *Mercury* assembled an astonishing lineup of talent prior to publishing the first issue. In addition to Rennolds, who lived in a renovated chicken house at the corner of Hermitage and Bellevue Roads near Bryant Park while serving as publisher for its entire run, cofounder Garrett Epps attended St. Christopher's School in Richmond and then graduated from Harvard, where he was president of the *Harvard Crimson*.

RPI graduate, *Proscript* and *Fan Free Funnies* alumnus and illustrator Bill Nelson was lured away from Richmond newspapers to work full time at the *Mercury*, and his distinctive, detailed cover illustrations and Virginia comics soon became regular fixtures. "All of us worked ourselves to death [that first year]," he told *Style Weekly*'s Deona Houff in 1989. "Everybody wanted it to succeed so bad until it not only hurt but ached."

Another Harvard graduate and *Crimson* alumnus, Frank Rich, came to Richmond to be the *Mercury*'s theater and film critic. "I had started talking about the idea of the *Mercury* with Garrett Epps and others," Rich said in the October 8, 2012 *Washingtonian Magazine.* "My connection to Richmond—besides Garrett, who was on the *Harvard Crimson* with me—was family. My aunt and uncle, Frances and Sydney Lewis, and their family lived there and were very active in the community. Richmond then was still a fairly sleepy town (except around VCU), operating at a Southern pace."

Columbia journalism graduate Harry Stein was recruited to the *Mercury* by his friend Frank Rich. "Frank's aunt and uncle were from Richmond and I didn't have a job," Stein said in a 2000 interview at the C-SPAN website Booknotes.org. "I didn't know exactly what I was going to do. And I got a call from Frank, who said, 'You know, these guys are starting this thing. You want to be a part of it?' I had nowhere else to go, so I ended up in Richmond."

Harry Stein's father, Joseph Stein, is the internationally known playwright who wrote the original book for the 1964 smash Broadway hit *Fiddler on the Roof,* among dozens of others before passing away in 2010.

Richmond native Robert Buford IV—former editor at University of Virginia's *Cavalier Daily*—became the entertainment editor. Lynn Darling (Harvard class of '72 and the lone female on the staff) was another former *Crimson* editor. Art director Peter Galassi put in so many long, brutal hours doing photography, layout and production that Frank Rich once commented that he didn't think Galassi ever left the building (Galassi did confess to crashing with Rennolds in his chicken house when he wasn't at the *Mercury*).

After a summer of planning, twenty thousand copies of volume 1, number 1 of the *Richmond Mercury* returned from printing at the *Fredericksburg Free Lance-Star* to the office at 16 East Main before hitting the Richmond streets on September 13, 1972. It was an impressive debut at twenty-four pages—a format to which they doggedly adhered for the first year, regardless of the number of ads. Charles Hite penned the cover story, entitled "Greetings from C&P: Buddy Can You Spare Another Dime?" It was an involved piece on public utilities regulation and the opacity of Virginia's telephone industry that set the *Mercury*'s standards for in-depth reporting.

On page 4, Harry Stein wrote his first article titled "Snatch," which was about the increasing shoplifting problem small businesses faced.

Frank Rich displayed his political chops with a commentary on page 6 entitled "Headaches and More Headaches: McGovern's Local Campaign Mirrors National Mishmash," about the amateurish George McGovern presidential campaign. "Somewhere in the Shuffle the mild-mannered

the richmond mercury

Inside:

Maybe elections by ward wouldn't be so bad after all. page 11.

The best of the New York Erotic Film Festival and Ladies Night in a Turkish Bath both promise a little more than they deliver. pages 16 and 22.

The first time Jim Miller saw Rod Stewart he thought he was terrible. Read why he changed his mind. page 18.

How Do You Tell a Polish Detective? On TV, he looks just like all the other detectives. page 20.

September 13, 1972   Volume 1, Number 1   Richmond, Virginia

Greetings from C&P

Buddy, can you spare another dime?

by Chuck Hite

Remember how you felt the first time you plunked a quarter in the Coke machine and got no change but only a can of carbonation in return? You'll probably feel the same way the first time you go to make a pay phone call and discover it takes not one dime but two.

That extra dime for a pay call is one of the ways that the Chesapeake and Potomac Phone Company of Virginia plans to extract more money—$36 million to be exact—from you, its customers. The nitty gritty of the process begins in a few days when C&P—one of a multitude of companies owned by the giant of the communications industry, AT&T—presents its case before the agency authorized to regulate monopolistic utilities in

Virginia, the State Corporation Commission.

You may shake your head about the proposed 20 cent pay call, just as you did about the Coke that cost a quarter. And you probably figure there's not much you can do about either of them. You may wonder if the telephone company really needs all that money. After all, didn't they get a $33 million increase in rates just last year?

Unfortunately, most phone customers, the rate payers, never get beyond the headshaking stage. Most may know that their rates are going up, but haven't realized the magnitude of the jump. In Richmond, for example, consumer phone bills would jump from $7.50 to $8.40 per month. Individual business lines would increase from $19.50 to $24.40 per month. Dialing a

continued on page 8

Richmond Mercury, volume 1, number 1, September 13, 1972. Art by Bill Nelson. *Courtesy VCU Cabell Library Special Collections, Richmond, Virginia.*

former WWII bomber pilot they are supporting for President this year has garnered the image of a 'radical' who would sell out the country to the communists and destroy the work ethic," he wrote. "This image is laughable to most people who know much about McGovern. But a lot of people know little more about the South Dakota Senator than what Nixon proselytizers spew forth on the evening news."

Pages 12 and 13 were the editorial pages, with a Garrett Epps piece called "Who's Afraid of Ward Politics" (about a possible return by Richmond government to the old ward system), and facing it on the right was a syndicated column by Jack Anderson titled "Chill in U.S.—China Thaw."

Lynn Darling debuted on page 14 with a piece called "Women in Richmond: The Light Begins to Dawn," about the lack of resources for women and women's groups in Richmond. It provoked a sharply critical letter from WGOE radio's Dave Austin, whose advertisement for a women's clothing store was censured by Darling in her article. "I suppose a new, avant-garde weekly includes a women's lib column for the same reasons a progressive rock radio station has to play records by Chicago," Austin wrote. "Well, good luck to the *Mercury*. There are still a few of us around who remember *The Sunflower*."

Pages 15 through 24 were review pages of films, books, drama, sports, TV, art and music. "The Pragmatic Gourmet" (written by a mysterious character named "Tantalus," who was actually Best Products CEO and Harvard graduate Andrew Lewis) reviewed the Fass Brothers Fish House, giving it "2 forks" in a review called "The Hushpuppy Is Alive and Well in Richmond." "Andy Lewis, as Tantalus, was the restaurant critic because he was the only one who could afford to go out and pay for a meal," said Slipek.

Frank Rich also reviewed the play *Ladies Night in a Turkish Bath* at Playhouse 3200 at the Holiday Inn West, claiming that "what it lacks in humor it resolutely fails to make up in flesh, and the result is a curiously pointless evening in the theatre."

Buoyed by this blistering start, issue numbers 2, 3 and 4 continued the irreverent, hard-hitting pace, featuring cover and interior stories such as "Younger Brother: The Sweet Life and Hard Times of Tommie Aaron" by Harry Stein (he considered this article on Hank Aaron's brother his best piece of writing at the *Mercury*); a piece on the state fair by Don Dale headlined "It's Madness as Usual When Carnies and Marks Get Together"; and "RMA's Highway Blues: Downtown Expressway Faces Uncertain Fate"—an in-depth look at the contentious and long-delayed Richmond downtown expressway boondoggle, written by Epps.

Twenty-five cents

Waiting for the water . . . and the dikes   page 6

the richmond mercury

a weekly journal
of news
and the arts

October 11, 1972   Volume 1, Number 5   Richmond, Virginia

The private faces of Bill Scott

There's more to the Republican senatorial candidate than meets the eye...much more

by Harry Stein

Bill Scott's former administrative assistant closes the heavy wooden door of the Capitol Hill office where he now works and faces the reporter. "You understand," he says, "that nothing I say can be for attribution. I've got a wife and family, and I can't risk losing my job over something like this."

The reporter nods. "Of course I won't use your name if you don't want me to. I'm primarily interested in your feelings about Mr. Scott and the sort of senator he would make."

The ex-Scott aide closes his eyes and inhales deeply. Then the words come in a torrent. "The man is the most morally corrupt individual I've ever known. There's nothing about him to admire. And I'm not talking about politics. Ideologically, I agree with him. I'm talking about the sort of man he is.

"His colleagues hate him. He's irascible, uncooperative and they avoid him.

"He's the cheapest man in the world. That story about him making his secretary wash rusty paper clips is absolutely true. He would wash out and dry toilet paper if he could.

continued on page eight

Richmond Mercury, October 11, 1972. Art by Bill Nelson. *Courtesy VCU Cabell Library Special Collections, Richmond, Virginia.*

"The *Mercury* did some of its best journalism in trying to get a well-rounded discussion of the downtown expressway and the environmental, historic preservation and the park's impact," said Slipek, "[because] it took out the playing fields at Byrd Park, and some 600 houses in Randolph, Maymont and Oregon Hill, and the *Mercury* was right on top of that."

But it was Harry Stein's cover story titled "The Private Faces of Bill Scott" in issue 5 that sealed the *Mercury*'s reputation as an upstart muckraker. In 1972, Senator William Scott was a conservative Republican from northern Virginia who was running against incumbent Democrat William Spong. Senator Scott was a very tempting target, as he was not well liked by his colleagues and certainly was not well liked by his former and current staff. Stein created what he later described on C-SPAN's Booknotes as a "vicious hatchet job," with Bill Nelson providing the unforgettable cover illustration of the senator sweeping a huge pile of dirt under a rug.

The article got mainstream local coverage, which was very exciting for this young group of "radical" college graduates. Stein said in the spring 2008 edition of the Manhattan Institute's *City Journal* that it was easy to portray Scott "as a mean-spirited, irredeemably incompetent nincompoop." "My Scott piece received ardent praise from colleagues and readers, proving, in case there was any doubt, that this kind of journalism had very little downside."

That article found life two years later at *New Times* magazine, where Stein and Frank Rich landed after leaving the *Mercury*. *New Times* rebooted the story as a cover by Washington correspondent Nina Totenberg, who prepared it both from Stein's old notes and from new interviews, calling it "The Ten Dumbest Congressmen" and crowning Senator William Scott "The King of Dumb." Enraged by the article and apparently recognizing Stein's name from the *New Times* masthead, the senator actually called a press conference to announce that he was not the dumbest man in Congress and that it was some sort of conspiracy of these left-wing punks from Richmond, Virginia.

"We had really done [Scott] a disservice," Stein told C-SPAN's Brian Lamb in August 2000. "And in retrospect, I regretted it, and it certainly made me reflect on my own behavior." Senator Scott was never able to shake the "dumb" distinction, and even his obituary in February 1997 cited the controversy.

"Since there was no money for marketing or advertising, the goal of the *Mercury* was to have one story a week that would make the evening news on its own," said Slipek. "It was 'The *Mercury* reported today that...' or 'According to the *Mercury*....' So that was the unofficial approach, and without that strength, the *Mercury* was not doing its job."

Toward the end of that critical first year, the most priceless movie review of all time appeared when the eminent Frank Rich went inside Richmond's infamous adults-only Lee Art Theater on Grace Street and reviewed an X-rated double feature. "If the Lee Art [Theater] is all come-on on the outside, it is, of course, all come within," he wrote in the November 29, 1972 issue. "On the screen men and women were demonstrating various methods of what used to be called self-abuse, and, from the auditorium, there was that tell-tale rustle of newspaper that suggested audience participation...The mystery adult hit ran only an hour, and at 2:30 PM the lights came up at the Lee Art—a signal, perhaps, that it was time to make room for a new crowd."

"When 'Bizarre Love Practices' began to unreel," Rich concluded, "a middle-aged man in a white coat came to my row halfway back from the screen and took a seat three places away from me. He had some weathered-looking newspapers under his arm which he soon placed in his lap. I heard a zipper being undone and decided it was time to take a walk."

In an unrelated story on page 4 of that same issue, headlined "Sirens of the Fan," Lynn Darling discussed with local residents the alleged reputations of VCU girls. "VCU girls? Yes, they have a reputation all right," said a University of Richmond student. "They're weird chicks, you know what I mean, they'll do anything."

By the end of its first full year, the *Mercury* was flying high and raising the journalistic bar, with ad revenues flowing. Almost every story was written by the same small number of staffers because they wanted no strict top-heavy hierarchy to "slow things down." There was no Liberation News Service or Associated Press stories in the *Mercury*—their only nod to syndicates was a Jules Feiffer cartoon on page 2 every issue and Jack Anderson's nationally syndicated column under that "Opinion" heading. In late 1973, they also ran Garry Trudeau's syndicated strip *Doonesbury*.

Buford's notion of the paper willing to "offend people" started by offending advertisers, beginning a long downward spiral of financial troubles that would eventually sink the paper. If a grocery store or a restaurant got a bad health inspection, the *Mercury* reported it, losing those advertisers. If a movie was bad, Frank Rich panned it (unusual in 1973 Richmond), and that soon cost them contracts with the former Neighborhood Theaters, Richmond's largest theater chain. "It was a battle every week with neighborhood theaters and Sam Bendheim Jr.," said Slipek. "For some reason, they got off on a bad footing."

While readers loved the paper, many local businesses weren't so eager to support a group of hotshot, Ivy League college-educated young liberals criticizing them, their beloved Governor Mills Godwin (the *Mercury* had endorsed Democrat Henry Howell for governor in 1972) or, worse yet, President Richard Nixon. Richmond unfortunately did not have an endless supply of replacement advertisers on deck ready to fill in the gaps created by the departing ones angered by the publication.

Also, it was tough up against the long-established daily papers. "There was no competing with the *Times Dispatch* [for ad revenues]," said Bill Kovarik. "They had advertising contracts built into retail rentals for most of the major malls in town. I sold advertising for the [*Chesterfield*] *News Journal* for a year, and I was told by many store owners that they already had their advertising quota soaked up in the *TD* contract, which was built into their store rental contract. That was monopolistic, but there wasn't much anyone could do about it."

The in-depth articles in the *Mercury* opened Richmond's eyes and certainly may have prodded the "complacent" daily papers to be more responsive to the community. Garrett Epps wrote a polarizing story about rapes occurring during a riot in the state penitentiary (then a grim building at Belvidere and Spring Streets), and Charles Hite broke ground about gay cruising on Grace and Foushee Streets, complete with a map of the gay "circuit" and gay slang—a problem Richmond would have rather seen buried. There was even a piece about how two high-ranking state officials spent three days at Port St. Lucie courtesy of Sperry-Univac just days before the state signed a $6 million contract with the computer giant. These were but a few examples of the high-quality investigative reporting that marked the *Mercury* that were somehow missed by the daily media.

But the *Mercury* wasn't all just hard-hitting, sometimes dour news stories; for example, VCU assistant professor Morris Yarowsky penned an analysis of the film art of local counterculture artist Phil Trumbo. "Trumbo takes apart the image structure of Child-dumb to reconstruct his own gloomy but hilarious world-view," Yarowsky stated in an article titled "The Films of Phil Trumbo" in the February 21, 1973 issue. "We are absurd Stoogians expressing love by bopping heads with rubbery brick-bats; messages come from above in planes, undulating phalli in the sky; things look good—but they are not!"

In 1972, Trumbo and Steve Segal made a remarkable black-and-white sixty-second stop-motion commercial for Mr. Moe's sub shops, with original music by Robbin Thompson and starring VCU theater student Stephen Furst (who starred as "Flounder" in the 1978 hit film *National Lampoon's Animal House*). "Trumbo has of course focused on the scatological innuendoes of eating those monstrosities," Yarowsky wrote of Trumbo's submarine sandwich experience, "and the expressive scene of this blimpoid food actually being eaten stands as a natural sequence to [the adult film] 'Deep Throat.'"

"I liked Morris but I think he was reading too much into my stuff back then," Trumbo said about that article in 2013. He and his partner Segal made that Mr. Moe commercial for $1,200 and paid the actors with bottles of wine.

From late summer 1973 until the beginning of 1974, the *Mercury* witnessed a succession of key resignations. Rob Buford left to take a public relations manager position at Richmond's Ethyl Corporation. Harry Stein and Frank Rich left for the *New Times* magazine that fall, and Garrett Epps left in January 1974 to take a succession of jobs as writer and/or editor for the *Richmond Afro-American*, the *Virginia Churchman*, the *Fredericksburg Free-Lance Star* and the *Washington Post*. He also began work on his groundbreaking novel, *The Shad Treatment*, which won the 1978 Lillian Smith prize for literature about the American South. Bill Nelson left to start his own illustration studio. "After the *Mercury*, I never worked anywhere else but went into business for myself," he said.

After the Harvard founding fathers departed, Glenn Frankel left the *Chesterfield News Journal* in November 1973 for the *Mercury* and stayed on until it folded in August 1975, claiming that the job made him see Richmond through eyes he had never used before. "Our journalism got more mainstream and less alt-weekly as it went along," Frankel wrote in 2012 of his tenure there, "mostly reflecting the personalities and aspirations of the individuals involved. Gene Ely helped move the paper more and more toward the mainstream, albeit with sharper-edged reporting and writing, throughout its final year."

Throughout 1974, the paper continued to expose corruption at Richmond City Hall and in the police force. A May 8, 1974 opinion piece titled "When Enforcers Become Instigators" described the Cherry Blossom riot of April 27 at City Stadium, which featured the music of the Steve Miller Band, Boz Scaggs and Dr. John. It decried Richmond as the city whose police "cannot keep their heads in a tough situation."

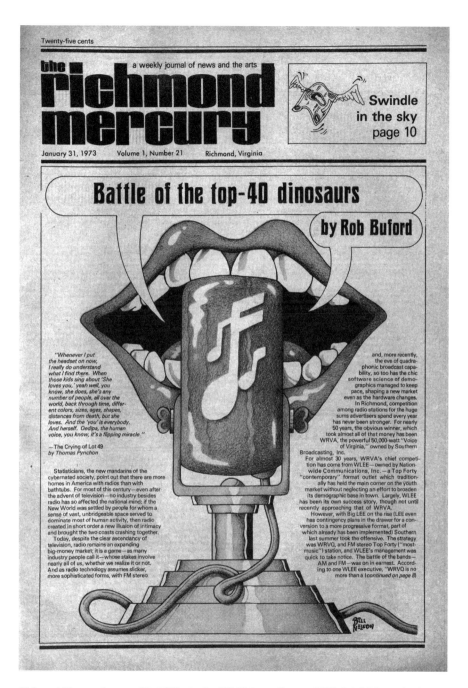

Richmond Mercury, January 31, 1973. Art by Bill Nelson. *Courtesy VCU Cabell Library Special Collections, Richmond, Virginia.*

The riot began as vice squad detective James Jackson attempted to arrest a man in the stands suspected of having drugs. A crowd of about fifteen spectators, objecting to the misdemeanor arrest after the promises that it would be a "hassle-free event," attempted to shield him. Jackson then brandished a pistol, which led to a rock and bottle free-for-all that lasted several hours, destroying ten city vehicles and damaging a building estimated at $50,000.

"[A] worrisome aspect of the confrontation is the thought that the rock festival disturbance was possibly engineered by the high command of the police department and the city administration in order to give rock concerts a bad name and prevent any more from being held in the city," an uncredited *Mercury* author speculated. "If one dismisses stupidity and inept police work as reasons for conflict between police and rock fans…then the only answer to why the confrontation happened is that someone let it get out of hand purposefully."

Several people were beaten by clubs and bitten by police dogs, including *News-Leader* reporter Bill Wasson, who was clubbed by a police sergeant. "A policeman was hitting [a youth] in a corridor," he told a *Times Dispatch* reporter, "and I tried to get the cop's name. Then I got hit." A picture of his bloodied, bandaged head appeared in the *Times Dispatch*. A WWBT-12 cameraman was bitten by a dog, and *Mercury* photographer Bob Strong was told by a police officer, "If I catch you pointing that camera at me, you'll eat it."

In the wake of the riot, the *Mercury* questioned the silence of city officials on the events of that Saturday, which led to the cancellation of the concert the next day that was to feature many black performers. "None have commented on what seems to be an escalating guerrilla war between the police and Richmond's hip community," Frankel wrote in the May 1, 1974 issue. "But the city is gaining national notoriety: It is the only American city where streaking has led to violence, and it now becomes the first in 1974 to have a riot at an outdoor music concert."

There were about one hundred arrests at the riot, most on drug and vandalism charges. Police major Russell Baughan told the *Times Dispatch* that he felt the policemen "did not go too far" in their attempts to quell the trouble.

"Streaking" was a short-lived 1970s fad in which persons or groups would briefly run naked through a public place before disappearing just as quickly. The "streaking" incident mentioned by Frankel occurred on the VCU campus on March 19, when a group of streakers riding in a convertible provoked a full-frontal assault by Richmond police, who charged into a festive crowd of onlookers, beating them with clubs and flashlights. Seventeen arrests were made, almost all of them bystanders. Despite a promise by City Manager Bill Leidinger that an independent investigation would be made into the streaking incident, an in-house investigation quickly concluded that the department had done nothing wrong.

Even after the 1974 personnel changeover, the reporting in the *Mercury* remained solid and still innovative as it continued to bleed money. Rennolds estimated that he and other investors, including the Lewis family, pumped $400,000 into the paper during its one-thousand-day run, and advertising revenues were not making up the difference.

"The business issues facing the *Mercury* cloud [its] memory in so many people's minds," wrote Gene Ely. "There was a huge amount of rancor among staffers about what was right about the magazine and what was wrong and why it failed, and the blame gets spread all over the place. The reality was that editorially it was a success from the start. Had the publication launched with the right business model, it would have been a great success, whatever editorial model was in place."

The money problems (and the hiring of unnamed "Editor X") from the spring of 1974 through its eventual demise in late August 1975 created a tense and sometimes intolerable situation around the newsroom. "Glenn was friendly, but Editor X was abusive, possibly because I was so green as a reporter, possibly also because of the stress everyone was under at the time," said Kovarik. "By abusive I mean screaming demeaning things, ripping my work out of my typewriter while I was still working on it, yelling things at me. It was bad."

"I was grateful, though, when I went to work for Jack Anderson in Washington in 1977, and I was able to weather the abusive atmosphere there and not take it too seriously, with the thought that I had already survived the worst."

"I'll offer one moment that meant a lot for me, if not the paper," said Glenn Frankel.

[In the fall of 1974,] *I was pursuing a tip about Richmond cops receiving payoffs to allow a pinball gambling network. I trailed a cop who went from gas station to coffee shop to gas station one afternoon. I was told he was serving as bagman. Afterward I phoned Commonwealth's Attorney Aubrey Davis, himself a former Richmond policeman. I told him what I'd seen and asked if his office was investigating. He erupted, told me he'd drag me in front of a grand jury to describe what I saw. I panicked, put my hand over the receiver and asked Gene Ely, who was in the room, what to do. Gene said "Ask him why he's threatening you." After all, said Gene, you're just doing your job. Immediately Davis started backing down. Said he hadn't meant it, was just kidding. Said he would look into the matter.*

Frankel said that he learned a great deal about the power and role of the press from that experience. "Even our little weekly had some leverage when we went out and did original reporting—something we felt the Richmond dailies were lacking. Gene's presence and determination helped push the *Mercury* further down that path toward a *Washington Post*–style mainstream publication that stressed good reporting."

Despite the ever-worsening financial problems, the paper doggedly continued breaking major stories, including one about illegal police wiretaps in Henrico County that prompted several resignations in Richmond's public works department. The paper questioned Governor Mills Godwin's trip in a corporate-owned airplane and asked tough questions of Virginia Electric & Power Company's rate structure. In May 1975, Ely wrote "A Night with the Klan," about visiting a KKK meeting down on south Richmond's Hopkins Road.

Finally, despite having subscribers from one-third of Richmond's estimated ten thousand college-educated households and ad revenues ticking up (ad rep Connie Abeloff scored some success in New York City with liquor companies and some other major accounts), the money simply ran out, and the August 20, 1975, publishing deadline was missed. Rennolds ("tired and despondent and looking more wrinkled than usual," according to Ely) called the staff together and announced that he and the other backers could no longer absorb the financial losses, which at that time totaled $500,000. The last paychecks were 60 percent of normal, causing quite a bit of bitterness among the staff.

"We relied on the small boutique advertisers, and when times are tough, advertising budgets are the first to be cut," said Slipek. "I think the Lewises had been putting money into the paper, but Best Products was also having some financial challenges because of the economy as well. Edmund [Rennolds] put his inheritance into it."

Temporary salvation came on August 20 when Richmond advertising executive Tom Laughon formed the Friends of the *Mercury* committee to raise funds and elicit community support for the beleaguered paper. He managed to line up about thirty potential backers, and Gene Ely resumed his post of editor and acting publisher. One more thirty-six-page issue was published (with an impressive twenty pages of ads) while options were studied, including finding a buyer or forming a new corporation. The staff worked without pay for two weeks, with the little money coming in used for rent and printing costs, but in the end, not enough funds materialized, and no one could continue on a volunteer basis. On September 4, 1975, the Associated Press reported that the *Richmond Mercury* had ceased publication for good.

"The overwhelming sense was of disbelief," Ely said in the 1989 *Style Weekly* article. "We had rocked along for so long, but in those last months we had started to grow; we thought we were really going to make it."

"When I got to Washington, this [*Mercury*] experience got me thinking that the alternative media was far too weak to be useful," said Kovarik, "[and] that I could work with more mainstream media, and I could feel at home because they weren't idiots like the editors I knew from the *Times Dispatch*."

Ely said that he was amazed it lasted as long as it did. "The longstanding rule of thumb for magazine launches was that just one out of ten would survive beyond the first year, and the vast majority of the titles that failed were launched by experienced magazine people."

"Edmund [Rennolds] was always trying to find a way to say yes and to balance these youthful forces, and month after month, he was beaten down but never lost his enthusiasm," said Slipek. "He was the last man standing."

The *Mercury* left an artistic, literary and journalistic legacy unmatched by any other alternative Richmond paper. Garrett Epps is professor of law at the University of Baltimore and has written (in addition to *The Shad Treatment*) four books. *To an Unknown God: Religious Freedom on Trial* was a finalist for the American Bar Association's Silver Gavel Award in 2001.

Frank Rich served for thirteen years as the *New York Times*' chief drama critic before becoming an opinion columnist in 1994. In June 2011, he joined *New York* magazine as writer-at-large. He has also written several best-selling books, including *The Greatest Story Ever Sold: The Decline and Fall of Truth from 9/11 to Katrina*.

Lynn Darling was at the *Washington Post* for eight years before moving to New York City, writing for various magazines, including *Newsday*. She also worked as contributing editor to *Esquire* and *Harper's Bazaar*. After leaving the *Mercury*, Charles Hite was a Pulitzer Prize finalist for his story in the *Roanoke Times* of life-and-death decision-making in an intensive care unit in 1991. Today, he is director of biomedical ethics for Carillion Hospitals.

Gene Ely is editor and publisher of Media Life Magazine, a website for media planners and buyers. Bill Kovarik is a professor at Radford University and in 2011 wrote the book *Revolutions in Communication*. Glenn Frankel, also a journalism professor at the University of Texas–Austin, recently released to wide acclaim his latest book, *The Searchers: The Making of an American Legend*.

Former *Mercury* artist and internationally renowned illustrator and sculptor Bill Nelson has won more than nine hundred awards, including two gold medals from the New York Art Director's Club. He has supplied numerous covers for *Newsweek* and the *Atlantic Monthly*, among others.

Harry Stein is an author and columnist, and in 1999, he wrote the book *How I Accidentally Joined the Vast Right Wing Conspiracy (and Found Inner Peace)* and in 2009 wrote *I Can't Believe I'm Sitting Next to a Republican*. He has been a contributing editor to the political magazine *City Journal* since 2000. Original production manager Peter Galassi has worked for more than thirty years as the chief curator of photography at the Metropolitan Museum of Modern Art. Edwin Slipek Jr. is highly regarded as Richmond's historical architecture expert. Rob Buford IV passed away in 1995.

Gene Ely said in 1989 that the *Mercury* found and celebrated a Richmond that was ignored by other media—that a publication like it should not only inform but also get people to think about themselves and become passionate about their communities. "We tapped into that passion because we shared in it," he said. "We dearly loved Richmond."

HANDBILLS, 1975—MID-1980S

They were dismissed as a nuisance, pollution and a hazard in the "public right-of-ways," but after the *Richmond Chronicle* folded in 1971, and before *ThroTTle* magazine started publishing in January 1981, the only means of widespread counterculture information dissemination throughout the city was by utility pole handbill posting, and mostly in defiance of creaky city ordinances.

Handbills and the "staple gun revolution" became Richmond's alternative print media of the 1970s. Early in the decade, local artists, musicians, writers, political pundits and anonymous troublemakers—egged on by the easy availability of a Selectric typewriter, a box of rub-on Letraset-brand letters, clip art, Zip-a-tone film, cheap local Xerography and a borrowed or a moderately-priced staple gun—began their own form of publishing in and around VCU and the lower Fan.

These were not just band advertisements, appeals for roommates and solicitations for guitar lessons; handbill posting during this period expressed a wide range of literary, musical and artistic genres. Topics and formats included announcements of indie film presentations, one-page social consciousness and arts newsletters and notices of art shows, poetry readings and performances. Sometimes they were free-form art that carried no message other than pure artistic expression. Many poles on Harrison and Grace Streets became so packed with handbills that they actually bulged at eye level.

"Early on, there were some types of people who wanted to do one-sheets, and it might have some diatribe on it—very rarely was it graphic-oriented,"

Above: Handbill Rally, 1982. Art and design by Doug Dobey. *Courtesy VCU Cabell Library Special Collections, Richmond, Virginia.*

Opposite: Save Oregon Hill Coalition handbill, circa 1980. Artist unknown. *Courtesy VCU Cabell Library Special Collections, Richmond, Virginia.*

Left: Drug informant warning handbill, 1970. *Courtesy Robert Mark.*

Opposite: Yard sale handbill, 1980. Art by Caryl Burtner. *Courtesy Caryl Burtner.*

said Rebby Sharp. "That began changing in the late '70s, where it became very graphic-driven, and I think Phil Trumbo had a lot to do with that."

In addition to Trumbo, there were a handful of artists, including David Powers, Terry Rea, Doug Dobey and Kelly Alder, whose graphic handbill work became instantly recognizable on poles.

"Dobey did [flyers] for the punk bands and the reggae bands," said Alder of the music-related handbills. "I did the rockabilly and the Americana bands, and Trumbo did the avant-garde bands. His were so much more sophisticated; they had a Jean Cocteau, Luis Buñuel, European surreal sensibility. I had to admit they looked really good. I thought why can't I do that?"

"Somebody else who did amazing flyers was David Powers," Alder continued. "He is one of the most brilliant people I ever met when it comes to just being creative."

"I remember admiring [Alder's] concert posters for the Richmond band the Bopcats stapled to telephone poles in the Fan when I was a student in the early 1980s," said artist Nick Schrenk.

By 1982, however, Richmond and especially the Fan District Association had decreed that handbills stapled to poles were officially litter. Musician and photographer David Stover was the first victim of the new law and was fined twenty-five dollars on June 28, 1982, for posting fliers for his band the Prevaricators. Charlie Williams and *ThroTTle* magazine advertising director Michael Woodall were then issued summons for posting a flyer for a Shockoe Bottom club. Aggravated by the crackdown, Biograph Theater manager Terry Rea—who had been using handbills since 1972 to promote films at the theater—intentionally got arrested to bring the handbill case in front of a judge after being confronted by a policeman with one of his own handbills advertising the film *The Atomic Café*. He later formed the Fan Handbill Coalition to address the crackdown.

Rea's case went to court on November 5, 1982. Attorneys John Colan and Stuart Kaplan argued that the city ordinance was not only overreaching but unconstitutional because it violated Rea's right of freedom of speech. Witnesses, including Phil Trumbo, retired VCU professor David Manning White and VCU art instructor Gerald Donato, testified that handbills had been a part of the American political, artistic and social communication process since colonial times. More than one hundred handbills were presented as evidence.

"I wanted to convince a judge that once you considered all the handbills in the neighborhood around VCU, it could be seen as an information system that some young people were relying on for information, just the same as others might rely on newspapers obtained from a box sitting on public sidewalk," Rea recalled recently on the *Biograph Times* website.

Assistant Commonwealth's Attorney William Bray argued that Rea could express himself and advertise the movies other than by posting handbills on public property, which, in a statement that stretched credulity, could also cause personal injury by falling off the pole, causing someone to slip and fall.

Donato lightened the proceedings when after several minutes of pointless back and forth, and frustrated at Donato's vague and intentionally high-brow answers, Bray finally asked whether a bunch of soup cans on the ground is art.

"Well," Donato replied, "it depends who arranged them."

"Making Punk a Threat Again" handbill, circa 1982. Artist unknown. *Courtesy VCU Cabell Library Special Collections, Richmond, Virginia.*

Ann Kay Gallery
handbill, circa 1982.
Art by Lynn Friel.
*Courtesy VCU Cabell
Library Special Collections,
Richmond, Virginia.*

Judge Davila dismissed the charge. The "flyer flap" then cooled until 1986, when Richmond again sought to prosecute offenders for posting. "*Slant* became a regular periodical on April 1, 1986. That's when I stapled the first ones to the telephone poles," said Rea. "And the handbill issue had come back—they had a new law." Rea, however, could not seem to get arrested this time around. "I wanted to get busted and couldn't."

"The handbills were a big part of that publishing culture," he said. "There were people who knew Kelly's handbills or who knew Phil's handbills or my handbills, who trusted those more than they trusted the *Times Dispatch*, so people would see a handbill for a band, for example, and even if they didn't know the band, they knew the artist who did the handbill, and they would go see the band based on that."

Left: *Stranger than Fiction* film premiere handbill, circa 1983. *Courtesy VCU Cabell Library Special Collections, Richmond, Virginia.*

Below: Mud wrestling at the Cha-Cha Club handbill, circa 1983. Design by Ray Bentley. *Courtesy the author.*

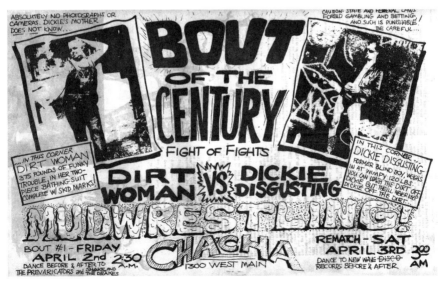

THROTTLE

The Magazine of Acceleration for the '80s,

1981–1999

ThroTTle *was a weirdly elegant Dixie-fried mongrel mix of the* Village Voice, Interview, Creem *&* Mad *magazine; a punk rock* National Lampoon *travel guide to proto-hipsterdom.*
—ThroTTle *contributor Ron Thomas Smith*

I feel that appearing in your magazine would be detrimental to me as a professional journalist.
—WXEX *channel 8 news anchor Janet Peckinpaugh, in a letter to* ThroTTle, *1982*

In December 1980, at the height of one of the worst recessions in American history, a group of recent graduates from Virginia Commonwealth University decided to publish a magazine. When the *Richmond Mercury* shut its doors after three years of weekly publishing in 1975, Richmond experienced yet another dearth of alternative literary and artistic media outlets. Once again, the *Richmond Times Dispatch* and *News-Leader* were the only games in town, with the exception of the monthly glossy *Richmond Lifestyle* and a couple of shoppers.

One of the largest and most prestigious art schools in the world was right in Richmond, yet there was no regular or frequent outlet for publishing the artists' works. VCU also had a booming creative writing department, a huge mass communications department and a fast-growing film and photography

ThroTTle, September 1983. Art by Kelly Alder. *Courtesy the author.*

school, yet other than the *Commonwealth Times*, there was not one publication in that entire city to display those talents. Like almost all alternative print venues, *ThroTTle*'s success was the confluence of these elements, coupled with a disdain for the current media monopoly, merging at the same time.

Two of *ThroTTle*'s three cofounders, Peter Blake and Bill Pahnelas, had a publishing history going back to junior high school students at Richmond's Tuckahoe, where they hand-published a mimeographed fanzine of art and prose called *Weirdness Plus*. Later, as VCU students, they took turns in various editorial positions at the *Commonwealth Times*.

In addition to their duties at the *CT*, Blake, Pahnelas and a handful of others, including Rob Sauder-Conrad, periodically published their own photocopied magazines, usually during spring and Christmas breaks, always at their own expense and just for the fun of it. *Mushroom Times* (May 1979) and *Spunk* (July 1979) were two of these efforts, offering exposure to poets, writers and artists they knew, in addition to their own contributions.

Finding common ground with the publishing prowess of his two senior editors with his own *Zip! Zap! Zowie!* comic books, cofounder Dale Brumfield gladly assumed the position of art director once former director Sauder-Conrad graduated, working not just on the *CT* but on a limited basis with the two of them in January 1980 for *Decade of Fear* (a title commemorating the election of Ronald Reagan), then later that May for a spring break publication called *Destiny*.

"This is the first and probably only copy of *Destiny*," Blake wrote on page 2, "but if you have any comments or contributions, we could possibly put them to use in our next as-yet-unnamed publication." That next as-yet-unnamed publication was initially conceived in a conversation between Blake, Pahnelas and Brumfield in the Stuffy's Sub Shop on Harrison Street in the summer of 1980, when one of them suggested they should do another magazine.

Peter Blake was reticent. "I don't know about that."

But Bill Pahnelas shot back, "Skeptics like you have held up progress for centuries!"

So, in December 1981, Peter Blake—feeling guilty for holding up centuries of progress—approached the others about publishing another independent magazine. At a planning meeting, they decided that this time they wanted a real magazine, possibly a full-size tabloid or broadsheet that they would be proud to carry to local businesses for distribution instead of having to sneak them in and hide them among the more respectable publications. They wanted to publish a significant number—a thousand or more—instead of the usual few hundred.

The group sweet-talked *CT* editor R. Steven Landes into letting them contract the use of the typesetting and Photostat equipment over Christmas break. Blake then ponied up the money needed to pay the Ashland *Herald-Progress* newspaper for printing one thousand copies of the inaugural issue of "unnamed tabloid publication."

Several names for this magazine were discussed: *Twisted* was liked by some, but it sounded too much like *Cracked*. *Mangle* was suggested, as was *Drive Your Car*. *Full Throttle* was a crowd pleaser, but since there was already a motorcycle magazine with that name, it was shortened to *Throttle*. The seemingly errant capitol *T*s in the final logo were the result of a typesetting error, but they were kept to stand for "Tough, Tenacious and Timely" (or "Torpid, Turgid and Taciturn"), although those marketing angles were never pursued.

The first issue of *ThroTTle* was an eclectic mix of fiction, news, humor, art and photography. The cover photo of a retro-'50s girl with giant pasted-on eyes and lips fondling car tires was lifted off a 1946 *Life* magazine. A centerfold story by Blake was about the grand opening of the brand-new Interstate 295 around Richmond, as well as a cruise taken by him and some friends in his pea-green 1975 Valiant. At the time, contributor Rob Sauder-Conrad had been the subject of a *Times Dispatch* article on his espousal of a half-serious movement called "Cruising for Peace," suggesting that if we all went cruising in our cars and burned up all our gasoline there would be nothing left to go to war over, ergo the article's title, "Twisted Tots go Cruising." Conrad even had T-shirts printed with the phrase "Cruising for Peace." This author started in that issue what turned into a yearlong *Lampoon*-like feature with "Tonight's TV," a compendium of fake analogue television listings.

Offered free of charge, volume 1, number 1 of *ThroTTle* magazine printed on January 14, 1981, in an edition of one thousand copies then delivered to various businesses around Richmond's fan district and VCU. Never meant to be sequential, it was published as a one-shot, just like all the others that preceded it. There were no plans at that time for a second one.

Unlike many similar alternative publications, where production was haphazard at best, the process behind publishing *ThroTTle* was highly organized. Type flow was tightly structured, with specific rules for editing and entering onto floppy disc. Hierarchy and deadlines were strictly enforced. Layout grid sheets were blue-lined and every headline, drawing and photo planned in advance. "The thing about *ThroTTle* was that while the ideas and look of the magazine were pretty wild, it was thoroughly professional as far as production and organization," said writer and former literary editor John Williamson in 2012. "Our monthly critique meetings were exacting, to say the least. Personal feelings were secondary to the target, and that was good."

It was serious business because, as Blake and Pahnelas stated a year later in a 1982 self-interview, if you impress with your personal integrity and professionalism, people will see you have credibility, "even if sometimes they think you are incredible."

"Everyone can talk about these trying economic times," Blake continued, "but they are also trying cultural and intellectual times as well. There continues to be in this city people who are interested in reading something beside what they read in the *Times Dispatch* and the *News-Leader.*"

Encouraged by the response to number 1, number 2 went to the printer on March 10, 1981, proving to Richmond that this was no pipsqueak upstart. *ThroTTle* slowly began organizing, breaking into defined sections and departments and going for the throat of Richmond's mainstream. The magazine needed money, however, and once again, when number 2 hit the streets, there still were no immediate plans to do another one.

Typical of the style of community participation that Peter Blake advocated for the magazine was his and Pahnelas's reaction to a blistering letter from former *Commonwealth Times* contributor Ron (Thomas) Smith. Unlike most alternative editors, Blake actually invited withering criticism, which he saw as critical to the magazine's success. While most of the staff dismissed Smith's letter as addled ramblings, Blake and Pahnelas responded as they knew best: they called the guy and asked him to write a column. Astonished that he was asked to participate in light of his disapproval, Smith remained a part of the magazine for years.

"You could say *ThroTTle* was a counterculture underground art magazine," Smith said, "but it was so much more than that. It didn't take itself too seriously yet was both visceral and cutting edge."

Since letters and submissions were rolling in, the staff felt that they were now obligated to keep publishing. As Pahnelas said, "We're creating a marketplace for ideas and an audience. Not so much as a conscious effort, but as a gathering of momentum."

Issue 3 was the last one to be wholly financed by the staff (mostly Blake) and the last one to appear without advertising. As soon as it hit the streets, Michael S. Fuller, former *CT* editor and the first guy the founders knew to buy his own microwave oven, joined the staff as business affairs director and promptly set about ways to raise the needed revenue. Ad sizes were created and priced, contracts were created and free layout and design services were offered for businesses that needed it. Fuller was a no-nonsense business guy who bluntly said that the magazine had no future without an infusion of outside revenue.

The entire staff hit the streets selling ads in one-hundred-degree Richmond weather in June 1981. A recession was on, and many hot and grumpy small business owners either had no money for advertising or had their ad budgets tied up in the Richmond dailies or in local shoppers like *Fan Advertiser* and *Fan Scan*. The grand total of ads sold for that issue totaled ⅝ of a page and netted about $135—a colossal first step in the direction of financial independence. To celebrate, the editors increased the press run to three thousand copies.

To make issue number 4 even more unique, graphic designers Ronnie Sampson and Nancy Martin came up with an idea to, in their words, "make *ThroTTle* more New Yorky." Hand-stapled on page 3 in one thousand of the three thousand copies was a second publication—a photocopied twelve-page three- by four-inch fanzine called *Subur-B-Q Magazine*, featuring tiny illustrations and flash fiction by such dependable Richmond creators as Lori Edmiston, Lisa Austin, Jean Hollings, "Art Mutt" and a few *ThroTTle* regulars. It was just another way to exploit talent and get more people involved in the excitement of publishing.

"*ThroTTle* was a boys club that I broke into," Lori Edmiston-Ellison recently wrote.

"How has advertising affected the magazine...," Bill Pahnelas wrote in February 1982. "Obviously, when we started, [we] had some ideas of where we wanted to take the thing, and when we took on advertising, it was a new situation where you'd have to worry about what the advertisers would accept and what the limits of good taste would be that they would buy into."

Pahnelas was justified in his concern regarding the limits of taste, but obviously the advertisers started buying into *ThroTTle* for what it was, not what they could make it, because number 5—only the second issue that contained paid advertising—was completely sponsored by those advertisers. *ThroTTle* was then off life support—a major milestone, reached in record time.

The fact that the magazine achieved its independence objective so quickly with no marketing plan, no investors and zero capital was a testament to the organizational work ethic of the staff, the talents of the contributors, the relevance the magazine capitalized on and the enthusiasm of the readership, proving how empty that niche was.

ThroTTle was not founded as an underground newspaper—exposing crooked politicians, calling for revolution against the "pigs," legalizing pot, ending a war or flaunting anti-obscenity laws. It never espoused the communal ideals or the radical political contingent inherent to the underground movement of the previous two decades. Realistically, that version of "underground" was nonexistent by 1981—coincidentally, the same year the Liberation News Service ceased to exist. *ThroTTle* was simply trying to fill a vacuum and have fun, not change the world.

In July 1981, this author sent a letter to Frank Zappa asking for a cover drawing after reading that he had performed an improvised piece at a 1972 show at Richmond's former Mosque titled "Why Do They Fry Everything in Richmond (Especially at My Hotel)." "Since your request is so utterly ridiculous," Zappa wrote back, "I will oblige you and I will draw something for you to use for your publication." His self-portrait on the cover of number 6, paired with an interview with filmmaker John Waters on page 11, closed out the magazine's first year with its first "celebrity" issue.

Self-portrait by Frank Zappa. *ThroTTle*, December 1981. *Courtesy the author.*

ThroTTle also closed out its first year in the black, financially—a miracle at a time when interest rates still hovered around 16 percent and joblessness at almost 10 percent. True, the magazine sponged facilities and machinery, paid no salaries and had almost nonexistent overhead, but it was a rare privilege for the editors to focus on the product and not on the finances.

Although *ThroTTle* may have started out in some readers' eyes as "underground," in February 1983, it cemented its reputation as a legitimate alternative arts and culture magazine when Anheuser-Busch wholesaler Brown Distributing signed on for a whole year of full-color, full back page Budweiser ads. The contract transformed *ThroTTle*; due to the printing press set up, there was no extra cost to print color on the cover, so suddenly a whole new world of dazzling, cheaply produced cover art opportunities opened, courtesy of a parasitic opportunity offered by Budweiser. The entire Richmond arts community got out its oils, pastels and watercolors, and soon *ThroTTle* sported eye-catching and socially relevant cover designs by such local and national luminaries as Kelly Alder, Gerald Donato, Anne Peet, Joe Seipel, Bill Nelson, Doug Dobey, Jim Bumgartner and others that may never have been obtained before.

The color changed everything. The magazine cut the cord with the *CT*, moved into a residential basement office and started publishing monthly. Professional photographers started calling, including then UPI photographer Bob Strong (formerly chief photographer for the *Richmond Mercury* and in 2013 senior photographer and editor-in-charge on the Reuters North America Picture Desk in Toronto), who shot spectacular pictures of idle construction equipment free of charge to accompany a story by Jack Moore. *Philadelphia Enquirer* Pulitzer Prize–winning editorial

Comic by Kaz. *ThroTTle,* June 1983. *Courtesy the author.*

cartoonist Tony Auth was more than happy to provide an illustration for an article on an execution at the state penitentiary. Cartoonists from New Jersey and California—including current *SpongeBob* and *Phineas and Ferb* artist Kaz, Peter Bagge (later a Harvey Award winner, creator of the grunge-rock comic *Hate* and temporary publisher of Robert Crumb's magazine *Weirdo*) and *Simpsons* creator Matt Groening—all started sending strips. Groening's strips, titled *Life in Hell*, were deemed too "amateurish" and sent back. (Yep. They were original Matt Groening strips. And they were rejected and sent back.) Shock rock band GWAR's cofounder Hunter Jackson submitted numerous comics featuring "Les Spivey," a sort of outer space punk rocker.

The press run steadily increased from three thousand copies at the end of 1981 to twenty thousand in early 1984, an almost unheard-of rate of growth for an independent unfinanced monthly publication in a town Richmond's size. By comparison, New York's most successful underground paper, the *East Village Other*, had grown from an initial press run of five thousand in 1965 to sixty-five thousand copies by the end of 1969.

Despite the presence of the Budweiser ad and the diversity of contributors, some of Richmond's mainstream media still saw *ThroTTle* as underground and a threat to their own legitimacy. In March 1982, newly hired WXEX-8 (now WRIC-8) news anchor Janet Peckinpaugh graced the final issue of *Richmond Lifestyle* magazine, and a *ThroTTle* staff writer wanted to write a feature article on both the death of *Richmond Lifestyle* and the hiring of Ms. Peckinpaugh. A friendly request for a mug shot of the news anchor resulted in a nasty mailgram from WXEX: "Strongly object to your proposed use of Janet Peckinpaugh's picture in your magazine—letter to follow."

ThroTTle then received a letter from Ms. Peckinpaugh herself: "After reading your letter and reviewing copies of your magazine, I am writing to inform you that you may not, under any circumstances, use my picture or name in connection with any story in 'Throttle.' I would consider such actions slanderous, libel, and an invasion of privacy…Most of all, I feel that appearing in your magazine would be detrimental to me as a professional journalist."

More threats followed, both from the WXEX station manager and from the station's law firm, May, Miller and Parsons:

> We must advise you that an invasion of the rights and/or privileges of Ms. Janet Peckinpaugh or Nationwide Communications, Inc. by the "Throttle" or any person or persons associated or producing or printing or participating in the invasion of either of our clients' rights will be looked to for full and complete compensatory and/or punitive damages.

> Signed very truly yours, G. Kenneth Miller, for the firm.

"The Throttle" responded as it knew best—by splashing the entire sordid affair on page 3 of the March 1982 issue. Artist Greg Harrison provided an accompanying illustration of Ms. Peckinpaugh punked out in spiked hair and leather jacket. The staff mailed copies to everybody involved, but the controversy died.

As harmonious as the magazine production often seemed, it wasn't always sweetness and light. Richmond movie mogul Ray Bentley never failed to either titillate or repulse with his garish one- and sometimes two-page midnight movie ads that were as much lurid feature articles as advertisements, and many staff members felt that the ads were misogynistic and sexist. Some felt that the magazine wasn't political enough, or too political, or that it devoted too much copy to the Richmond music scene. Some complained that the humor and art were tasteless and too "National Lampoonish." One comic artist wrote in asking who he had to perform oral sex on to get his strips published. "You don't have to [redacted] anybody," answered comics editor Doug Dobey, "just draw better strips." Arguments sometimes broke out over money, cover art or last-minute story inclusions and editing changes, a "bad habit" that especially drove Bill Pahnelas crazy and sometimes caused bad feelings that lasted for days.

Then, on October 26, 1983, someone with really bad feelings broke into the offices at 7 East Broad Street and destroyed the place. Tables were overturned, art supplies thrown everywhere and a $600 printer was thrown into a light box, demolishing them both. As a final exclamation, the culprit(s) used the floor as a toilet. Thankfully, the Apple IIE computer was left alone, or the magazine would have been out of business.

"As much as alternative journalism bound us in a way, the actual practice separated me from them just as much," said contributor Ned Scott Jr., who later became editor in 1987. "It was a constant culture struggle…I was tired of arguing about content and thought the magazine was spending too much space sucking up to local bands."

"I volunteered to proofread and spent hours finding typos, believing I was earning the privilege of doing a cover," said Richmond artist and frequent contributor Caryl Burtner, "and finally I was promised the June 1984 cover and I planned to show 'Bride of Xerox,' and I was so excited until I found out at the last minute that the art director had given my cover to a VCU professor."

In October 1983, *ThroTTle* was the only Richmond media outlet to publish an in-depth story about poet and longtime counterculture contributor Rik Davis, who was murdered at his job at B&T Adult Bookstore at 1203 West

Broad Street the previous April. The April 11, 1983 *Richmond News-Leader* stated that the apparent motive for the attack was robbery.

"[Davis] has outdone me," Davis friend and fellow poet Lester Blackiston told *ThroTTle*'s Donald C. Wilson. "This gentle, sweet fool Davis killed by some poor bastard who thinks so little of life that he'd take it from someone else…Do they want poetry to come out of the fucking mud?" As of 2013, Davis's murder is still unsolved.

By 1984, *ThroTTle* had incorporated under a subchapter S company called Acceleration for the Eighties, Inc., which issued stock worth one dollar a share. Bank accounts were created, loans were signed for equipment purchases and the corporation acquired Channel 36 Coloradio, an independent radio station that broadcasted over the color bars on Continental Cablevision TV's blank channel 36. This author and Rob Sauder-Conrad scrounged local dumpsters to accumulate enough lumber to build hinged-lid layout tables as the organization moved downtown over top of the Neopolitan Gallery.

Shortly before moving into 7 East Broad Street, *ThroTTle* started an internship with Richmond's Open High School, in which four students would get high school credit for working at the magazine. One of those original interns, Michele Houle, wrote in 2012, "My first involvement with *ThroTTle* came after I wrote a letter to the editor, which led to a 'teen perspective' piece. That fact alone, to this day, is a source of great pride. Not that whatever I wrote was any good, but that I was a part of this amazing thing."

Another original intern was this young lady in denim bib overalls who at age fifteen quickly assimilated and wrote with the maturity and wizened sarcasm of someone twice her age. Timmie—or as she is also known, Anne Thomas Soffee—is today a regular columnist for *Richmond* magazine and the author of the books *Nerd Girl Rocks Paradise City* and *Snake Hips*.

"The first *ThroTTle* staff meetings I went to were at Dale Brumfield's apartment on the Boulevard," said Soffee. "For me, it was like sneaking backstage with my favorite band. I tried to act like it was no big deal, but I was actually totally star struck. I remember going home and calling my friends to brag that I'd met Caryl Burtner and Kelly Alder."

Soffee and Andy Marcus scored an interview with Black Flag lead Henry Rollins in September 1985. "Every time I got an assignment, I felt like I'd won something," said Soffee. "In my own head, I was Lester Bangs."

ThroTTle maintained a strong readership among the young people of central Virginia. In a May 24, 1983 *Richmond News-Leader* article, a group of New Kent High School students named *ThroTTle*, along with *Cosmopolitan* and *Seventeen* magazines, as their main influences for their "new wave" clothing styles.

"I grew up in Midlothian in the 1980s," said Syracuse University professor Greg Geddes. "To go down to Plan 9 [Records] was a huge treat, and my friends and I read *ThroTTle* whenever we could get a copy. For a teenager with little access to other media than the *Times Dispatch*, it was like a lifeline."

"*ThroTTle* was a big reason I decided on Richmond when I left [high school]," said Richmond artist and musician Wes Freed. "I had a copy I picked up at Back Alley Disc in Charlottesville. I read that issue cover to cover several times. That was where I first heard about Beex and White Cross."

Other literary and musical highlights of the mid-to-late 1980s included interviews with fiction writer William Crawford Woods, illustrator Berni Wrightson, the Bad Brains, singer Grace Jones, the Ramones, REM, cartoonist Colleen Doran, Richmond musician Dika Newlin, Dream Syndicate ("A hilariously scroungy piece of writing inspired by a scroungy band in a scroungy business," wrote Trent Nicholas in a letter to the editor of Donna Parker's interview), primitive artist Howard Finster and '60s relic Tiny Tim. Film culture experts Nicholas, Dave Harrison and Terry Rea contributed numerous film commentaries and reviews on little-known films like *Liquid Sky*, *Taxi Zum Klo*, *Napoleon* and the Phil Trumbo/Steve Segal "world's smallest epic," *Futuropolis*. Ben C. Cleary, Dabrina Taylor and John Williamson headed up a strong literary department that provided learned commentary on the newest local and national book releases, including even Dr. Seuss's *The Butter Battle Book*.

"I remember I wanted to meet [artist] Bill Nelson, so Greg Harrison and I devised this scheme to interview him for *ThroTTle*," recalled Kelly Alder. "And that was my way to break the ice and meet him, and he gave us this great image to use on the cover."

"Of all the publications I recall, *ThroTTle* was my favorite," wrote University of Richmond Writing Center director Joe Essid. "I was more drawn to the punk scene in a grunge sort of way than to the other subcultures of the era. There was a lot of creativity in the air of the Lower Fan then, and a good deal of angst about the Reagan years. I've never gotten over my anger kindled by the radicals I met, and I thank them all for it."

"*ThroTTle* was halfway down the rabbit hole," said frequent contributor David Powers. "It kept me from being totally lost, and no one would ask, 'What are you doing here?'"

But like almost every magazine before it, as fast as *ThroTTle* climbed, it began an equal but opposite descent. No independent alternative publication

"Top Teen" feature by David Powers. *ThroTTle*, November 1982. *Courtesy the author.*

in Richmond had ever reached its five-year anniversary before, and no one knew what happened next. Advertising began dropping off, and contributors and staff members faded, tired of almost five straight years of unpaid grunt work. The 1986 summer issues may not have had enough advertising to pay for themselves, but not publishing at all would have been even more financially disastrous.

Then, at an August 1986 board meeting—just as the directionless magazine reverted back to its birth weight of eight pages—the editorial and production regimes changed. Bill Pahnelas was already gone by then due to a no-compete clause at his job, Peter Blake was burned out, this author was burned out and getting married and Coeditor Jeff Lindholm was burned out and moving to Charlottesville. Not wanting to see the magazine go under, former contributor Ned Scott Jr. met with Peter Blake to discuss plans to basically start all over with a fresh new focus and a new staff. This was a no-brainer to the founders.

"Be careful what you wish for," Scott reported. "When I showed up at the office [in 1986], I was almost knocked over by the old regime heading out the door. They weren't happy that I had the paper, but they were ecstatic that they didn't. They all seemed tired of the grind, and it showed up in the pages of the magazine."

Ned Scott Jr. was aggressive, loud and demanding but an excellent writer and editor, and he had high hopes for taking *ThroTTle* into the 1990s with the same rough-and-tumble enthusiasm that had marked its acceleration in the 1980s.

"Rounding up a new staff took a bit of cajoling," said Scott, after moving the offices into his own apartment on Grove Avenue, "and even though diplomacy isn't my strong suit, I managed to get enough talent to launch a credible first issue. With that over with, it was arguing once again with the few old regime lingerers and the new staff about content: having a horoscope ended up with longer conversations than conversations about political articles."

"When Ned took over as publisher, he wanted to go more news-oriented," said graphic designer Doug Dobey in 2012, "and he asked me to be art director, and I was really excited about it. I redesigned the logo but kept the two prominent capital *T*s in the middle. I did a sort of constructivist cover that was bold, with red and white. But what bothered me was that Ned wanted to start news on the front page…and for years and years, *ThroTTle* had this coveted cover, and it was a big, big deal getting a *ThroTTle* cover. I always felt guilty about being the person who did that."

ThroTTle, January 1987. Story by Ned Scott Jr. Design by Doug Dobey. *Courtesy the author.*

In January 1987, *ThroTTle* came off life support. Scott had done a near-miraculous job cajoling a new staff of writers, artists and photographers, and they created a twenty-page issue highlighting the AIDS epidemic. It had beefier arts and sports coverage, and Brown Distributing was on the back page again. It was a miraculous rebirth under dire circumstances.

Still, the production remained contentious. Scott said that it slowly dawned on him that Richmond had the readership to support *ThroTTle*, but the advertisers still weren't eager to be seen in the pages of it. "It would be easy to blame that image on the old guard, yet the truth is that the space between the readers and the retailers was too great for any real alternative magazine to survive, and *Style* (a monthly publication then) was offering a far safer advertising venue."

By the end of 1987, Scott had left, and longtime staff member Dorothy Gardner took over as editor. Dorothy and her ex-husband had been important parts of the magazine for two years, filling a variety of production and sales positions, and she presumed herself qualified to run the entire operation.

"Ned left, and it was like, 'Oh gosh, who is going to take over?'" said Ann Henderson, who later served as senior editor from late 1988 until the final issue in 1999. "Mary Blanchard and I were doing a lot of work, but we were too shy to take it over, but Dorothy said, 'I'll do it,' so Dorothy was editor for a year or so."

It was a difficult year, and in September 1988, Gardner was forced out by the staff due to editorial and business differences. No longer shy about their leadership skills, Henderson and Blanchard took over and promptly moved the offices back to downtown Richmond, just around the corner from the old 7 East Broad location.

"We moved to this really rough space on the corner of Foushee and Broad Streets—there was pigeon poop in the corners, and we had space heaters. It was owned by a guy who was running a kung fu school. And we were getting rent discounts by running ads for his kung fu school."

Despite the recent turmoil and the less-than-ideal working conditions, veterans and new contributors were still attracted to the magazine and continued to hang around the dirty, barely-heated space, doing paste-up, listening to music and drinking Black Label beers simply because it was fun. "I went to one *ThroTTle* staff meeting...feeling intimidated, fearing that I would be the lone dork in a room full of ultra-hip hipsters" said musician Paul Ivey. "It was a relief to arrive and find a table full of some of the nerdiest folks in human history. I thought, 'Oh—MY people!'" Henderson and Blanchard fostered a positive working environment as coeditors by splitting the responsibilities, with Henderson doing the editorial work and Blanchard the production.

"It was perfect poetic justice when Mary and Ann gave me the honor of making art for the back cover for nearly seven years," said Caryl Burtner. "And how many of my ideas would never have come to fruition without having the page in *ThroTTle* to produce?"

At this time, the magazine took a one-year break to reconsider the direction the new staff and leadership wanted to take. "That is when we changed to the smaller size," Henderson said, switching the layout from

ThroTTle, July 1993. Art by Pat Wittich. *Courtesy Ann Henderson.*

standard tabloid to eight and a half by eleven." Artist Pat Wittich redesigned the logo, and printing was moved from the *Fredericksburg Free Lance-Star* to the *Hopewell News*.

After resuming a bimonthly production schedule in early 1992, the staff needed more creative ways to keep the finances solvent. They gave up the dreary space on Foushee Street and moved production into Ann Henderson's apartment. "Finances were always such a struggle," she said, echoing a tired old Richmond story, "and as we were figuring out the printing bill, Mac Calhoun, Mary and I would figure out how much money we didn't have and divide it among the three of us and say, 'OK, we can print if we each put in sixty-seven dollars.'"

Soon, though, the magazine found a way to defray most of the out-of-pocket staff expenditures. "We always ran record reviews," said Henderson, "and once we started sending tear sheets of our record reviews to the record companies, especially the alternative college radio stuff, they would send us more CDs to be reviewed, and they started running ads with us. So we would sell the CDs they sent us to Plan 9 Records. The relationships with these small record labels saved us."

The magazine also had marginally successful benefit shows at a club called Rockitz at Laurel and Broad Streets (the location of the former Free University performing arts center). "They were fun, but it was stressful. We wouldn't make much money, but it was good promotion for the magazine."

ThroTTle still offered excellent feature stories that never strayed from its countercultural roots. A January 1993 issue featured a cover story by Ceci Costanzo on 1970s hip fashion, foreseeing 2012's resurgence of those horrid clothes by almost twenty years. Another 1993 issue featured an interview by Todd Ranson with David Lowery, of the alternative rock band Camper van Beethoven. The Holiday 1997 cover story, titled "98 Years of Virginia Weirdness" by Scott Burger and Carol White, highlighted such juicy Virginia oddities as the story of Andrew Dickson, a Norfolk man who minted his own coins from silverware and had been in business ten years when police finally caught him in 1936. Contributor Kevin Kravitz continued a long tradition of having his picture taken with celebrities, and that feature appeared throughout the '90s. Cartoonists Seth Feinberg, Don Bone, Lynda Barry and Shade Wilson continued to contribute their spectacular artwork.

As the stress and cost of publishing grew more acute and contributors had shorter and shorter shelf lives, the magazine soon went from bimonthly to quarterly, barely quarterly and sometimes down to once or twice per year. "There were people who wanted to contribute, but the hard work of putting it out was falling more and more to me and just a couple other people," said Henderson, before echoing every editor who ever came before her. "It was the burnout factor."

It is a testament to the staff, contributors and advertisers that *ThroTTle* stayed around long enough to experience firsthand major printing technological advances, going from typed hard-copy stories, waxed galleys and mechanical paste-up in the early days all the way to onscreen pagination using PageMaker software on home computers—an advance that also had a dark side. "At first, people would turn in their articles on floppy disks," said Henderson, "but then as people started turning in things by e-mail, I found people got sloppier with their writing. Things like that were making the work even harder." While there were still a handful of loyal contributors—like Scott Burger, Christopher Hibben, Phil Ford, Lynda Barry and a few others—almost all of the actual production fell on Henderson, with Mary Blanchard assisting when she was available.

In early 1999, after almost a year-long hiatus, the staff agreed that it was time to end it all. There was increased competition for readers and advertising dollars, and most importantly, there was no next generation of staffers willing to knock themselves out for the joy of seeing their work in print when the relatively new concepts of website publishing and blogging were gaining popularity. The final issue of *ThroTTle*, number 156, came out just before Christmas 1999 after a remarkable run of almost nineteen years, a record for an independent freestanding Richmond publication wholly staffed by volunteers. The final issue contained retrospectives on some of the more unforgettable writers, artists, photographers and even advertisers who appeared within the pages over the years.

"[Before] our final issue, we had not put one out for like a year," said Henderson, "and on the last issue, there's a big typo on the cover…it was like, 'OK, it is time to stop doing this.'"

"One of the great things about *ThroTTle* was it was a steppingstone for a lot of people," said Dobey. "I know for me it was—I was doing work for this incredible free publication, and there was that rush of seeing the thing printed…and I discovered how much I love publications. I was at *Style Weekly* and *Richmond* magazine after that in art director roles, so I owe a lot to that little magazine."

"In some ways, I think the spirit of *ThroTTle* still survives," said contributor Phil Ford. "Richmond is just a town that has this odd and wonderful dynamic that lets a lot of creative people express themselves in a lot of different ways. Today, it happens to be a bit more splintered into subcultures and scenes. *ThroTTle* managed to bring them all into one big heaping place, one issue at a time."

In January 2000, *Richmond Times Dispatch* writer Mark Holmberg lamented the magazine's passing in a column titled "*ThroTTle*'s Death Leaves Void in Underground": "Adherents to Richmond's tired and trite reputation as a fossilized southern town have long ignored our unusual and often outrageous underground cultural scene, a scene that was revealed and celebrated in *ThroTTle*. The burning question: is it just *ThroTTle* that died, or does its passing signal a dissipation in our underground art and music scene?"

SMALL PRESSES

In Richmond, and specifically in the Fan District, the art and the music and the characters back then were just as cool as any city. We just weren't in a media center. [But] when it comes to starting up magazines, everybody's got one magazine in them. But the question is, can you sustain?
—*artist and publisher Terry Rea, January 7, 2013*

Richmond's alternative small press and its espousal of an even more personal form of nonobjective publishing during the '70s and into the '80s often reflected some more eccentric values of the counterculture. While a few hard-nosed small press publishers rejected the alternative press with the same vigor as the dailies, resistance to or rejection of the "established" alternative wasn't always their sole purpose; most seemed more willing to supplement the existing alternative media with their own voice to simply clarify or enhance the niche, not replace it.

With little or no access to professional printing outlets, and sometimes little to no financing, Richmond's small radical press library grew quickly, and numerous offset or photocopied publications appeared in a variety of genres. Some lasted one or two issues and some lasted for years, but all of them are fascinating glimpses of their objectives and the environment that spawned them.

HAPPENINGS, 1973

Happenings, November 1973. *Courtesy Jim Drewry.*

Happenings was one of Richmond's first independently produced alternative news and information publications, first appearing on the streets around the Fan District in September 1973. Edited by Jim Drewry, *Happenings* said that it "hope[s] to answer that every weekend question of 'What's going on tonight?'"

Happenings noted in the introduction on page 2 of the first issue that it was "written about Fan people by Fan people," and, "It is not sponsored by the university or backed by any big money"—a possible swipe at the VCU-sponsored *Commonwealth Times* and the *Richmond Mercury*, the latter of which was at least partially backed by theater critic Frank Rich's uncle and aunt, Sydney and Francis Lewis, founders of Best Products Catalog showroom.

More than just a calendar of events, *Happenings* also showcased the various idiosyncrasies and colorful residents of the Fan. Writer Sue Snaman profiled pottery artist and former staff member of *The Sunflower* Emily Galembeck as she prepared for a one-woman show at Chelsea Court in Watergate East. Issue number 6 featured a cover story on John G. Robertson, who sold flowers at the corner of Boulevard and Kensington Avenue for thirty-nine years.

Happenings published about nine issues, finally ceasing around January 1974.

The *Grassy Knoll Gazette*, 1977

Published quarterly at 903 West Grace Street by Artifacts Records president William Burke and Associate Editor Ralph Holmes Jr., and with contributions by R.B. Cutler (of Manchester, Massachusetts), this newsletter studied America's fascination with presidential assassinations and took a hard look at the circumstances, inquiries, investigations and conspiracy theories surrounding them. "The editor knows too many people, friends and such, who are interested in these assassinations, and are skeptical, to say the least, of the findings of the 'official inquiries' into them," said a full-page introduction in volume 1, number 1.

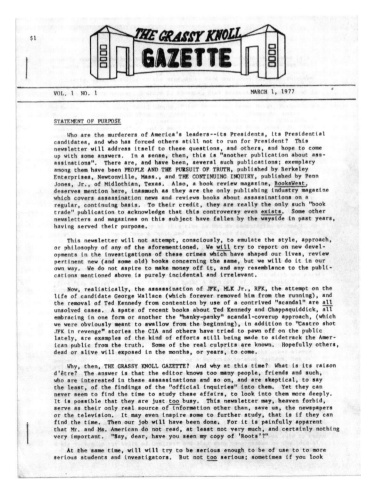

Grassy Knoll Gazette, March 1977. *Courtesy Steve Wall.*

Features include items about political assassinations culled from other publications, reviews of various Kennedy assassination literature, charts and analysis of the infamous Zapruder film and a sporadic column called "Dealey Plaza Breakdown." A culinary arts column by "Harker Goody, Esq." included recipes, like "Harker Goody's Real Texas Cross-Fire Chili."

RICHMOND NEW RAVER, 1978

Quite possibly Richmond's first alternative music publication coinciding with the city's eminent punk rock movement and the growing handbill "staple gun revolution," *Richmond New Raver* was created and published by musicians David Stover and Tom Applegate, with a single issue appearing on May 22, 1978. Weighing in at a substantial sixteen pages, *RNR* sought like all preceding Richmond music magazines to garner some attention and publicity to the local music scene that was growing too fast to be

ignored, printing stories, lyrics, a few photos and blurbs about both local bands and national acts appearing in Richmond at the time, including the Ramones, who played at the VCU Halloween Dance that year.

Richmond New Raver, May 1978. Photo by Chris Forrester. *Courtesy Caryl Burtner and David Stover.*

RAW-O-METER (AND RAW-O-GRAM), 1978–80

Richmond Artists Workshop was formed in the summer of 1976 by musicians Danny Finney and Pippin Barnett as a consortium and support group of artists and performers, and in 1978, it rented space and became "official" at 1717 East Main Street in Richmond. Its first function was a poetry reading on August 3, 1978, and throughout the remainder of the '70s, it sponsored literary, music and art performances from two to four times per month. Barry Bless and Tom Campagnoli served as presidents.

"Danny and Pippin sent out flyers for a meet-up at Monroe Park for people interested in forming an artist co-op or workshop," said Campagnoli. "That morphed into RAW."

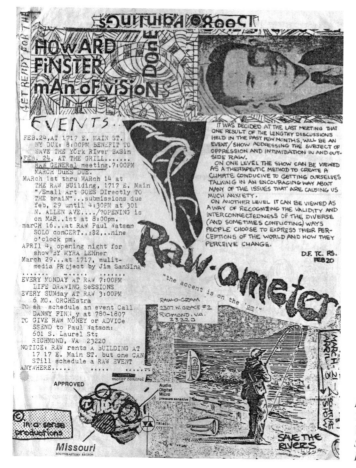

Raw-O-Meter, circa 1979. Courtesy VCU Cabell Library Special Collections, Richmond, Virginia.

The various *Raw-O-Meters* and *Raw-O-Grams* served as communication vehicles, publishing calendars, announcements and news pertaining to the group and to the arts in Richmond. They were works of art in themselves, typically 1980s collages of text, found objects, clip art and original art.

An "End of the Seventies" *Raw-O-Gram* edition published in January 1980 included in its '70s chronology music performances by such Richmond luminaries as Duck Baker, Sunset Lou and the Fabulous Daturas, Eugene Chadbourne, the David Orcutt Blues Band, Half Japanese and Idio-Savant. Art shows by Rebby Sharp, Julie Copeland, Paul Greenberg and Mary Crenshaw were also included, as were several other dance performances and poetry readings.

In 1982, RAW gave up the East Main Street space due to a "lack of funds and a lack of energy," according to codirector Holly Sears in a January 1983 *ThroTTle* article.

Both the *Raw-O-Meter* and the *Raw-O-Gram* were distributed free of charge around the Fan and downtown.

Mushroom Times (May 1979), *Spunk* (July 1979), *Decade of Fear* (January 1980), *Destiny* (May 1980) and *Rockets & Weenies* (July 1980)

Between May 1979 and July 1980, VCU *Commonwealth Times* editors Peter Blake and Bill Pahnelas, along with a few others—including Rob Sauder-Conrad, myself, Jack Moore and Ronnie Sampson—published a total of five one-shot photocopied publications, each with its own theme and focus and each in an edition of between one hundred and five hundred copies. Clandestine production was maybe done in the *Commonwealth Times* offices at 916 West Franklin Street, and printing was usually done by the VCU print shop or Lawyers Printing.

All of these little magazines were only meant to give the creators a chance to showcase their own work and the works of others in differing formats, be it short fiction, news commentary, reviews, art, satire, poetry, photography or even nonsense. They were, however, produced in a professional manner, with the exception of the Fourth of July celebratory magazine *Rockets & Weenies*, which foreshadowed the 'zine publishers of the twenty-first century with its eclectic and sometimes incoherent mix of photos, found objects, clip

Mushroom Times, May 1979; *Spunk*, July 1979; *Decade of Fear*, January 1980; *Destiny*, May 1980; and *Rockets & Weenies*, July 1980. *Courtesy the author.*

art, rub-on Letraset-brand letters and blurbs about, what else, rockets and weenies—American Independence Day fixtures.

Most of these publications tried to offer explanations for why they existed. "*The Mushroom Times* was thinking when it picked its name," said the *MT* introduction on page 2. "We chronicle the living rise of growth from the rotting log of America in all its ramifications."

Destiny was a little more truthful about the employment situation of its creators. "Talk about Destiny. Sometimes we just don't have anything to do. We don't go to school, we don't work…"

Decade of Fear was cautiously apprehensive of the coming Reagan years. "So now that we find ourselves on the edge of a new decade, what are we supposed to do? How do we make it, put our own personal stamp on it to let future generations know we did stuff other than just go to sock hops and wear poodles like they did in the Fifties…?"

Spunk offered no reasons for existing.

After the publication of *Rockets & Weenies*, the following December 1980, the same group decided to publish another magazine—only instead of becoming a one-shot like all the rest, this one lasted for 156 issues over nineteen years. They called it *ThroTTle*.

THE BEAT, 1980

"*The Beat* originated during a conversation with Dudley [Holland] about music in Richmond," noted the introduction in issue 2 written by Editor Mark Brown. "We realized there was a great need for a publication to cover the original music and events that were happening around the city."

With that, musicians Mike Ventrella, Steve Vaughan and Brown, all members of the recently defunct band Naughty Bits, decided to address the lack of entertainment coverage provided by Richmond's establishment press. The first issue of *The Beat*, with the assistance of copy editor Steve Vaughan, art director Lori Edmiston and layout editor Mike Ventrella among others, appeared in September 3, 1980, and sold for twenty-five cents on Fan newsstands.

The Beat, October 1980. Art by Frank Gresham. Design by Lori Edmiston. *Courtesy the author.*

"We went to Manchester High School together and had all worked on the school newspaper," said Brown. "Mike had an underground paper, too, called *The No Bull Sheet*, that also took root at Midlothian High, where artist Frank Gresham, Gary Walker and Aimee Mann went."

There were two issues of *The Beat*. Cover art was by artist and filmmaker Frank Gresham on issue 1 and by Doug Dobey on issue 2.

"The Heretics loved our description of them," said Brown. "Music to Shave Cats to." He continued: "*The Beat* was put together by a lot of cool people who I'm happy to say are all still friends of mine."

THE *NEW SOUTHERN LITERARY MESSENGER*, 1981–87

Created at 302 South Laurel Street by Charles Lohmann in January 1981, the name was adapted by Spencer Adams from the 1840s Richmond magazine of the same name that had been edited for a period by Edgar Allan Poe. Appearing quarterly and selling for fifty cents, the *NSLM* contained poetry and prose poetry, flash fiction and satire contributed by Lohmann and "the unrecognized and the unknown," according to issue 4. The spring 1983 issue published the first color cover, provided by artist Carol Schwarzman and the Richmond Printmaking Workshop, which produced several covers that year. In the summer of 1984, Lohmann announced in the preface that he would publish only Richmond-area poets "for very good reason": "It will make it easier to attend publication parties and drink for free."

In the spring of 1987, Lohmann called it quits. "It is now as good as I can get it and to continue it or make it better I would have to form a staff and find a lot of money for wages," he wrote in the preface. "[But] like any honest, creative work, it gets better as you grow with it."

RALEIGH REVIEW, 1981–84

Originally founded and published by the VCU School of Social Work in 1976, this "independent journal of social affairs" broke away from the

Raleigh Review, spring 1984. *Courtesy Peter Blake.*

university in 1981 and was published quarterly by an anonymous staff consisting of "social workers, social activists and assorted others concerned with social change."

"The *Raleigh Review* seeks to address issues of relevance to Richmond and Virginia with a mixture of investigative journalism, editorial commentary, poetry, plagiarism, humor and all-around lack of good taste."

Content was mixed: the spring 1984 issue contained a serious interview conducted by Kent Willis and Bruce Cruser with Virginia civil rights pioneer (and publisher of *The Ghost*) Dr. Edward H. Peeples Jr. ("The Unmaking of a White Supremist [*sic*]"), yet it also ran an elaborate six-page parody of *ThroTTle* magazine, called *Toddle*. Letters to the editor were obviously made up.

HARDBALL, 1982–87

As if the creators of *ThroTTle* magazine did not have enough to do putting together a fast-growing monthly tabloid, they decided that because of the huge influx of unsolicited contributions, they would create a second magazine to give even more contributors a chance to be recognized. With that, they published the first issue of *Hardball*, "a Magazine of Acceleration for the Eighties."

Hardball was a broadsheet filled with dozens of short stories, poetry, commentary, submitted photographs, original artwork, comics, clip art and ephemera. With longtime *ThroTTle* contributor Michael Clautice acting as editor and production manager, the first issue appeared in October 1982 and was self-supporting through paid advertising. Five issues were sporadically published until 1987.

SOUNDZINE, 1983

A true underground publication in almost every gritty way, six angry, arrogant, frequently filthy and always hilarious issues of *Soundzine* appeared between May and December 1983. But behind the "Bricks and Tomatoes" (the opinion column on page 2) were serious and insightful looks into the inner workings of Richmond's amazing and fast-growing music scene. *Soundzine* was enormously supportive of Richmond bands, clubs and club owners, giving kudos where they were due and savaging the "posers and wankers" when it was deserved.

Founded by Brooke Saunders and a cast of Richmond "music morons," the "most erratic publication in Richmond" was an unapologetic mix of photos,

Soundzine,
number 5, 1983.
*Courtesy Brooke
Saunders.*

clip art, typed interviews, drawings, random musings and miscellaneous
noise clipped legally or not from an endless variety of sources. "I was
inspired to create *Soundzine* because of *ThroTTle* and other publications
coming out around town," said Saunders in 2012. Art contributors included
band members Tom Rodriquez, George Reuther and Bobby Crockin. Steve
Hunter was a contributing writer.

An unforgettable interview with Richmond's infamous celebrity "Dirt Woman" (Donnie Corker) in the June 1983 issue offered Dirt explaining why in a local gay bar he "sprayed a dozen drag queens in the face with mace": "Me and some queens got into a fight," Dirt explained. "I told that girl [a drag queen] not to hit me and she did and I hit her with tear gas in the face."

Saunders explained, not surprisingly, that "we got a number of complaints from businesses about the content—not to mention an offended citizen or two."

Soundzine attempted to publish monthly, with the price jumping from free to fifty cents to seventy-five cents to whatever was needed to cover printing and distribution. "The only promise we make is that you will get a new issue every month," read a subscription ad in the June 1983 issue. "We can't say when, why, where or how—we're about as regular as Dirt Woman's periods."

Soundzine's staff enjoyed the perks of publishing. "I read a review of the Dave Brockie/Death Piggy issue in a British zine, who called it one of the best they saw that year," said Saunders. "Getting into shows and other special events for free because of our press status was fun," he continued. "We went to the 9:30 Club in D.C. and got the red carpet treatment."

Saunders added that seeing *Soundzine* "for sale at a yard sale" was the highest honor he could get.

Not the Green Section and the *Richmond Inquirer*, 1984

Not the Green Section was a one-shot publication produced by this author in March 1984 that was a line-for-line parody of the *Richmond News-Leader*'s Saturday entertainment insert, *The Green Section*, complete down to the green wraparound cover. *NTGS* included fake feature articles about a Hollywood film made in Richmond and a Performing Arts Center that suddenly and inexplicably exploded. Inside features included the "Richmond-on-the-Tollbooths" spring walking tour schedule and a detailed TV listing, with such shows as *Art Linkletter's Keg Party* and *My Three Reruns*. Movie guides and even ads satirizing real Richmond restaurants appeared. One thousand copies of *NTGS* were printed by the *Fredericksburg Free Lance-Star* newspaper, and they were snatched up for free from local Fan businesses after people caught on to what it was.

Not the Green Section and *Richmond Inquirer*, March and September 1984. Written and designed by Dale Brumfield. *Courtesy the author.*

"My roommate picked one up, and I saw it on the coffee table in our apartment," said Fan District resident Anne Fleischman, "I thought it was the real *Green Section* so I threw it away."

Brumfield and the paper were the subjects of a good-natured April 17, 1984 feature article by Harriet McLeod in the real *Richmond News-Leader*, titled "Not Serious."

Bouyed by the success of *Not the Green Section*, Brumfield then created the *Richmond Inquirer*, a parody mash-up of the *Richmond News-Leader* and the *Weekly World News* the next September.

"It's almost like the real thing."

CLUE, 1984

In the summer of 1984, alternative publishing specialists and *Richmond Mercury* veterans Edwin Slipek Jr. and Rob Buford IV decided that

Clue, August 1984.
Photograph of Suzy
Peeples by John Henley
and Chuck Savage.
Courtesy Edwin Slipek Jr.

Richmond was ready for a different kind of magazine. Armed with some discretionary funding from their public relations careers and their numerous contacts in Virginia's arts and entertainment industry, they formed the Company Corporation and started work on *Clue*. Published quarterly, *Clue* sold for two dollars.

Clue was based on Andy Warhol's *Interview* but got its name from a monthly gossip column that Slipek wrote for *ThroTTle* magazine. "[The column] was total foolishness, but I carried that format over to a personality-driven publication," Slipek said. "One thing spawned another." The staff and editorial board was a who's who of the Richmond culture and counterculture community, with such familiar names as Garrett Epps, Jerry Lewis, Edmond Rennolds III and many others.

Oversize and glossy, *Clue* appeared at the time in Richmond when the Sixth Street Marketplace opened, and "there was an orgy of civic pride and enthusiasm in downtown," according to Slipek. The publication's intent was to combine the establishment of which he and Buford "had ironically become a part" with the culture, music and the arts that reflected that urban enthusiasm.

"Rob Buford and I took all the people we knew, in business in the arts or entertainment. We got interesting people interviewing interesting people. We wanted to be a little bit sexy and see where it went."

Despite the strength of its content and production, *Clue* lasted only two issues. "I started my own public relations business," Slipek said, "and it struck me that journalistically it had no integrity. I would be too tempted to put my clients in. So we stopped."

Even though the magazine did not last long enough to build an audience, Slipek reported that both issues sold out. One hundred copies of the Phillip Johnson cover issue "flew off the shelves" at New York City's Palace Hotel.

SLANT, 1986–93

In late 1971, Richmond native Terry Rea was offered what he considered "the best job in the Fan District," that being manager of the brand-new repertory Biograph Theater at 814 West Grace Street, a baby sister to Georgetown's Biograph Theater, which had been opened by the same group of investors in 1967. On February 11, 1972, Richmond's Biograph opened with a champagne party and the 1966 Genevieve Bujold and Alan Bates comedy *King of Hearts*.

Whereas the Lee Theater had defined and enhanced Richmond's counterculture community in the '50s and early '60s, before it became an adults-only porn theater in 1965, the presence of the Biograph and its eclectic mix of offbeat film offerings helped define and enhance the countercultural VCU/Grace Street community throughout the '70s and '80s.

With the help of original assistant manager Chuck Wrenn, in-house ad campaigns were implemented befitting the somewhat antiestablishment movies that had box office potential. Offbeat radio ads on WGOE, a popular

Slant, volume 1, number 1, June 1985. Written and designed by Terry Rea. *Courtesy Terry Rea.*

AM station with a heavy hippie audience, and (for the first time) hand-drawn handbills by Rea were posted on utility poles and bulletin boards around the Fan District and VCU.

Throughout the '70s, however, the Biograph encountered the same problems the Lee Theater had almost twenty years earlier: Richmond simply was not an art house film town. Foreign and art film packages, such as Luis Buñuel's Oscar-nominated *The Discreet Charm of the Bourgeoisie*, performed wonderfully at the Georgetown Biograph but did poorly in Richmond. What boosted the theater's finances, however, was pornography: seventeen consecutive weekends of the infamous 1972 porn film *Deep Throat* at midnight grossed more box office cash than eight weeks of Bergman and other foreign offerings. A subsequent showing of another first-run adult film, 1973's *The Devil in Miss Jones*, grossed even more than *Deep Throat* despite a legal injunction that stopped the film from being shown after several sellout screenings. As a prank, at the height of the legal proceedings, the theater screened a 1941 RKO potboiler titled *The Devil and Miss Jones* with a Disney short called *Beaver Valley* to an enormous and unsuspecting crowd. National Public Radio's *All Things Considered* program the next day compared the hoax to Orson Welles's *War of the Worlds* radio program.

Throughout the '70s and well into the '80s, the Biograph Theater and Rea (then later Mike Jones and Tom Campagnoli, who took over as managers in 1983) maintained a close relationship with the Richmond arts community and especially the independent print media. The Biograph was always a reliable advertiser and distribution point for the *Richmond Mercury*, *ThroTTle* and some of the other small press publications. In turn, screenings for such offbeat or little-known films as *Liquid Sky, Polyester* (with director John Waters in attendance), the locally made and produced *Futuropolis*, the Talking Heads film *Stop Making Sense* and the restored 1927 *Napoleon* received extensive write-ups in those publications, hopefully driving audiences both to the print media and into the theater. Many Biograph employees were also contributors to the alternative print media of the time, and some even created their own publications. For example, longtime Biograph employee Tom Campagnoli cofounded the comics journal *Boys and Girls Grow Up*.

Terry Rea also started his own publication after leaving the Biograph. "By the time I quit the Biograph in the summer of 1983, I had gotten addicted to thinking I had a readership that wanted stuff from me," he said in 2013. In 1985, his alternative paper *Slant* debuted, printed in 1,000 copies and selling for twenty-five cents. The next issue, number 2, was printed in 2,000 copies, but Rea considered it a failure because it only sold 1,300 copies.

Going literally back to the drawing board, Rea introduced *Slant* a second time on April 1, 1986. "That's when I stapled them to the telephone poles [because of] the handbill issue—I had gone to court and won and was looking to do it again. It came out twice a week, Tuesday and Friday, and the first one was one side with ads on the bottom. By the second, I had copy on the front and the back, so I had to put one on one side of the pole, and the other on the other side."

After three months of handbill distribution, Rea switched to a newsletter format, mostly to protect his regular advertisers from Richmond's new handbill law. "The law was such that the advertisers could get busted [by being on a pole], that whoever benefited from the handbill could be busted too. I felt there was no way that could be legal."

Devoted to Rea's political causes, local history, softball and to life in the Fan District, *Slant* changed format almost every year. "It was a tabloid for a while, it was a newsletter, it was folded six different ways...a typical-looking *Slant* depends if you picked up the first year or the fifth year," Rea said. *Slant* was published weekly until 1987, when it switched to a sixteen-page tabloid with a peak press run of eight thousand copies. Shortly after that, it went back to handbill size, around five thouand copies and given away for free.

In 1993, Rea "burned out," and his son-in-law set him up with a blog, which he dubbed "Slantblog" "for lack of anything better."

Rea remembered one particular moment delivering *Slant* to the Fan Market on Robinson Street that was pivotal to him. "I heard this lady pick one up, and she seemed not at all like a person who would read an alternative publication, and she waved it and said, 'You want to know why I read this?' and I'm thinking okay, you got my attention, and the cashier said, 'No why do you read it?' and the woman said, 'Because it makes me feel less crazy!'"

POETIC RICHMOND (1982) AND POEMS OF NEW BOHEMIA (1983)

"We'd like to mobilize the bohemians here," a cheerful, Bible-quoting self-described "bohemian mobilizer" named Roger Coffey told *Richmond News-Leader* arts columnist Roy Proctor in 1981. "To pull them out of the closet."

After serving as a United Methodist minister, a radio preacher and a life insurance agent, Coffey reinvented himself in the early '80s as a patron of Richmond's literary counterculture, dedicated to the bohemian spirit of Richmond's Fan District. Coffey offered the Grove Avenue Gallery (which he "founded in the spirit of romantic idealism" with local artist Richard Bland) to artists and his own printing operation to the local writers.

Poetic Richmond, 1982. Art by Richard Bland. *Courtesy VCU Cabell Library Special Collections, Richmond, Virginia.*

"We want to become a regional cultural center in the South with a national outreach through our publications," he said of his patronage. "We want Richmond artists and writers to be better known, here and elsewhere." Coffey was especially willing to help Richmond's poetry community gain exposure, through small press poetry collections and monthly poetry readings at the gallery. His first published collection, *Poetic Richmond* (1982), featured poems by twenty-eight notable Richmond talents, including John Alspaugh, Cassandra Cossitt, Rik Davis, Charles McGuigan, Eddie Peters and many more. Richard Bland provided the cover art, and layout and design were by V.D. Phillips.

Poems of New Bohemia (1983) followed the next year, with new works by many established talents, as well as new talents such as Joe Essid, Bill Beville and Brenda Emroch.

A staunch anti-nuclear advocate, a veteran of more than one hundred demonstrations and an Independent candidate for Virginia's Third District House seat in 1984 (losing soundly to Republican Thomas Bliley), Coffey also authored two political essays in the booklet *The New Revolution* (1983), an international statement dedicated to the advocacy of human rights and one dedicated to nuclear freeze. "Where have the radicals who marched and protested against the Vietnam War gone?" He asked in the booklet before answering himself: "Most now have good jobs and are part of the system."

Caution! The Illiterati Magazine of Richmond, 1989–92

Published by Mauricio Cordero, along with Editors Tim Meinbresse, Dave Wiseman, Marc Black and Juliet Guimont, *Caution!* was a photocopied and folded legal-size arts publication that appeared for four issues, seeking to showcase various Richmond artists and writers. "We wanted a forum to show our work," said Juliet Guimont. "We used to have *Caution!* parties, where we'd have bands play, poetry readings and, of course, kegs of beer. This would help pay for the printing costs."

"I believe Charles Bukowski had something published in one of the last two issues," Guimont added. Local contributors included C. Maynard Bopst, Bill Hill, Anne Hart, Carol Hahn and other Richmond talents.

Caution!, 1990. Art by Bill Hill. *Courtesy Julia Guimont.*

OTHER SMALL PRESS OFFERINGS

In 1968, the VCU Arts Union published several issues of *Mirror*, containing news and events of the brand-new VCU School of the Arts. Printed like a true mirror—text was printed backward on the back, requiring a mirror to read—the news sheet reported the union's large aspirations, stating at the top of issue number 4 that they were formulating plans to invite to VCU such luminaries as Andy Warhol, Robert Motherwell, Marshall McLuhan, Art Kane and other figures in the art world.

The *WCA Newsletter,* published by the Richmond Women's Caucus for Art, appeared in December 1978 and contained issues pertinent to women in the arts.

Mr. Donut, self-billed as "probably the most totally stupid mag in Richmond," was created in the mid-'80s by shock rock band GWAR cofounder Dave Brockie. It published at least two issues of comics, short fiction, art and reader contributions.

"We are not a normal record company," read the introduction on page 3 of *Artifacts,* a catalogue produced by Artifacts/Yclept Records president William Burke in 1981. The *Artifacts* catalogue was actually even less a catalogue than an offbeat advertiser for the bands included, with graphically appealing ads inviting readers to contact the musicians directly to make purchases or inquiries. "It's a catalog that should have been a magazine," wrote Peter Blake in *ThroTTle* magazine about *Artifacts.* At least three issues printed, and the striking grayscale cover on issue number 1 was by David Gregory.

COMICS JOURNALS

GRAPHIC SHOWCASE, 1967, 1969, 1970

In the fall of 1967, right around the same time Art Dorow and his staff put together the first issue of *The Sunflower*, a Richmond comics aficionado named Tom Long, along with art director Jim Traylor, assembled an impressive lineup of comic artists to produce Richmond's first comics journal under the name *Graphic Showcase*, published by CCAS Publications and selling for one dollar per copy.

"Getting together a first issue is always somewhat of a problem," wrote Long in the folksy, self-deprecating editorial in the first issue's inside cover. "Even though it is a labor of love! Love it has to be since it is from the sweat of your brow or a hot, flaming, pulsating piece of your own flesh!"

Pulsating flesh and blood aside, the first edition of *Graphic Showcase*'s forty-four pages featured the amazing talents of some of Richmond's best young comics artists, including Michael Kaluta, Steve Hickman, Steve Harper, Johanna Bolton and a high school student named Michael Cody. "Cody is a great admirer of the Marvel bullpen," wrote Long in the introduction, "so look out Stan. This fella is a prolific penciler."

Tom Long was a committed fan of the "old school" style of comics and was a prolific comic storyteller and script writer himself, itching to produce his own publication. "I didn't buy my first several fanzines; I was lent them by Tom Long," Kaluta told the website comicattack.net in 2010. "I was introduced to Tom by my pal Mike Cody while I was in my first year of college [at RPI]. Mike thought my comic strip, 'Eyes of Mars' [that] hung on the bulletin board in our local alternative book store and music venue, the Scarlet Griffin, would be a swell addition to Tom's proposed publication."

Despite the success Long experienced with the first issue, it was two years before issue number 2 finally showed up in the summer of 1969. "I think you'll agree the long wait was worth it!" Long boasted on page 2. "And I don't like to brag, but I, personally, think it's the greatest collection of art to ever grace the pages of an amateur magazine!"

This wasn't idle boasting—the second forty-six-page edition was indeed spectacular. Another color front cover by Michael Kaluta and a color back cover by Steve Hickman surrounded black-and-white interior strips, including *Veneficium Malificarum* by Hickman and Kaluta, *Captain Infinity* by Long and Hickman and an eight-page strip called *Uncle Bill's Barrel* by an amazing non-Richmond newcomer named Berni Wrightson. Although it wasn't the very first appearance of Wrightson's work, it was considered by many to be his breakout work that went on to establish his stature in the comic illustration world, leading years later to great acclaim with his signature comic *Swamp Thing.*

"[Wrightson] drew better than anybody I'd ever seen that was that young," said Kaluta.

The third and final issue of *GS* appeared exactly one year later in 1970, featuring a color cover illustration called "Spy Smasher" and a back cover called "Sandman" both by (non-Richmond) sci-fi artist Gray Morrow. In addition to Morrow and the regular artists Kaluta, Cody and Hickman, this issue also featured the work of Phil Trumbo, Charles Vess, Alan Simons and Kenneth Smith.

In number 3, Long announced that numbers 1 and 2 had sold out, and a final 250 copies were reprinted and sold for $1.50 each before the plates were "disposed of."

Every story in *GS* was a dazzling example of sequential storytelling, and every artist featured went on to become a nationally known comic artist and illustrator—an incredible track record for a small home-grown publication and a real testament to the conviction of the publisher and his ability to recognize and showcase unique talent.

One of the artists in particular, Phil Trumbo, was not just a contributor to *Graphic Showcase* but was also a giant in the Richmond art and counterculture scene, beginning in 1966 as a student desperately trying to fit into the RPI art school mold under Richmond arts pioneers Theresa Pollak and Bernard Martin. "I did cartooning in my sketchbooks but in art school I was doing art school paintings," Trumbo said in a 1981 *Commonwealth Times* interview. "I was doing post-Abstract Expressionist-Hans Hoffman-influenced stuff. But my heart was really in cartooning."

Trumbo lived in the same cluttered second-floor Grace Street apartment almost his entire tenure in Richmond, surrounded by twentieth-century American pop ephemera, including mannequin heads, 1950 stuffed chairs, Salvation Army lamps, tin toys, paperbacks and comic books ("years of haunting Goodwill and Hull Street"). Trumbo was Richmond counterculture personified, not just with his interior decorating skills but also via his art, animation talents, filmmaking and as bass player in an avant-garde rock and roll band, the Orthotonics.

Trumbo's tireless work in those early publications paid off. "[In 1977,] I approached *Heavy Metal* in New York, which was originally just the English-language version of *Metal Hurlant*," he recalled. "I really just wanted to do covers, but when [Editor] Julie Simmons saw my stuff, she liked it and said, 'Do us a strip.' So I did *Exquisite Corpses*, a tribute to the surrealist parlor game."

Trumbo interviewed his friend Kaluta in *Comics Journal* number 103 in 1985. "If there were three people in Richmond who were as enthusiastic about the comic medium as [Tom Long], then you'd see something as terrific now as *Graphic Showcase* was terrific in the '60s," Kaluta said, recalling the influence of the journal. "Since growing up, I've looked at the fanzines that came out that same time, and the stuff being drawn then was just a touch underneath *Graphic Showcase*, surprisingly. A noble effort, nobly executed and with absolutely the best reproduction ever in that time period. And certainly it was a venue for me. The people who mattered to me saw my work there."

Many of *Graphic Showcase*'s artists have won too many awards to count and are still going strong. Michael William Kaluta may be best known for his work on the series *Starstruck* and *The Shadow*. He has done dozens, if not hundreds, of science fiction covers, illustrations and comics, with work appearing in Marvel Comics, DC Comics, *Blast* magazine, *National Lampoon*, *Heavy Metal*, *Amazing* and *Fantastic Digest*. In 1971, he won the Shazam Award for outstanding new talent and in 2003 the Spectrum Grandmaster Award, as well as many others. Not so widely known is that Kaluta created cover art for the 1973 rerelease of Bobby "Boris" Pickett's novelty album *Monster Mash*. Kaluta also designed the illustrations and directed the animated music video for the 1984 Alan Parsons Project song "Don't Answer Me," which included the talents of Richmond artists Kelly Alder and David Powers. It became one of the most requested videos of the year on MTV.

Stephen Hickman is a fantasy and science fiction illustrator who has won a Hugo Award from the World Science Fiction Convention for the U.S. Postal Service's space fantasy commemorative stamp booklet. He has also won five Chelsea Awards from Science Fiction and Fantasy Artists. He has illustrated more than four hundred book covers for Bantam, Doubleday, Ace and others, and in 1988, he wrote *The Lemurian Stone* for Ace Books, which went on to form the basis for his *Pharazar Mythos* illustrations.

Michael Cody was a longtime illustrator for Medical College of Virginia Hospitals (now VCU hospitals) and provided illustrations for children's magazines and artwork for Edgar Rice Burroughs fanzines. World Fantasy Award winner Charles Vess's art has also appeared in *National Lampoon* and *Heavy Metal*, with other work published by Marvel, Dark Horse, DC and Epic. Vess also collaborated with writer Neil Gaiman on the illustrated novel *Stardust*, which went on to become a Paramount Pictures movie in 2007 starring Robert De Niro and Michelle Pfeiffer.

Phil Trumbo is an award-winning art director, designer, concept artist and animation director, providing creative direction to nearly one hundred high-profile video games for Electronic Arts and previously for Broadcast Arts, Hidden City Games and Amaze Entertainment, among others. He designed the initial concepts and the opening sequences for the TV show *Pee-wee's Playhouse* and won an Emmy Award in 1986 for creating and directing that sequence. He has been nominated for three Clio Awards and is the author of the graphic novel *Sky Pirates of the Stratosphere*.

"I got my Emmy award in the mail, and it came broken," Trumbo said. "It looked like some production assistant threw it in the box with no packing."

In 1972, Tom Long ventured again into publishing with the oversize *Tom Long's Americana Comix*, featuring twenty-four- by thirty-six-inch reproductions of classic multipage strips by Basil Wolverton, Jack Cole and Joe Simon. He passed away in Richmond in 2010.

Fan Free Funnies, 1973

In the fall of 1972, newly appointed *Commonwealth Times* executive editor Edwin Slipek Jr. made the decision to showcase some of the art school's amazing graphic artists in an attempt to appeal not just to the student body but also to the Fan District and Richmond community at large. With the help of fellow editor Stephen Lasko, editorial cartoonist Mac McWilliams and local artists Phil Trumbo and Charles Vess, Slipek created a comic supplement to the *Commonwealth Times* in February 1973 called *Fan Free Funnies*.

"It struck me that if I was interested in going a feature direction [with the *CT*], then why not engage more artists, and this is where Charles Vess and Phil Trumbo came in," said Slipek. "I had put out a call for writers, cartoonists and illustrators, and when there were lots of illustrators but not that many folks from the journalism side, I said, 'Well, let's do a supplement to showcase their work.'"

Phil Trumbo was a natural to help organize such a collection. As cofounder of the Richmond Artists Co-op, he influenced many of his artist friends into contributing full-page comics to this *CT*-sponsored enterprise. He came up with the name and provided the distinctive color illustration for the first cover.

"*Fan Free Funnies* was really a diverse collection, representing vastly different graphic styles and inventive, experimental approaches to sequential storytelling," Trumbo said, citing the work of 1960s underground cartoonists like Robert Crumb, S. Clay Wilson and others, including such old-school artists as Walt Kelly, as influences.

"I gave Phil a ride over to the printers," Terry Rea recalled about preparing Trumbo's color cover of the first issue, "and on the tissue paper overlay, he would outline an area, and write '10' or '12' for color from a PMS ink chart...and Phil named every color. And it was fun doing it."

"Phil Trumbo was very, very aggressive about wanting this publication to happen," said Slipek, "because he was so extremely talented and extremely supportive of his fellow artists."

Only three issues of the *Fan Free Funnies* were produced. Inspired by the underground artists as much as by early 1970s *Lampoon* and *Metal Hurlant*–style artists like Moebius, Claveloux, Sherry Flenniken, Vaughn Bode and J. Jones, there were no real rules as to the content of the contributions; artists in all three issues utilized largely experimental approaches to their comic storytelling, drawn in their own markedly distinct styles.

Fan Free Funnies, number 3, summer 1973. Art by Damian Bennett. *Courtesy VCU Cabell Library Special Collections, Richmond, Virginia.*

Fan Free Funnies number 1 was sixteen pages, with two and a half pages of paid advertising, including a one-fourth-page ad on the back cover for a free concert February 14 at the VCU New Gym featuring Dan Hicks & His Hot Licks, with as their opening act a little-known performer named "Bruce Springstien."

The VCU Media Board bristled at the idea of publishing a comic paper. "Oh, they were furious," said Slipek, "because we just went on and did it because to me it was just like a sports supplement or a dining guide, but it was so out of left field and it seemed perfectly natural to me. I saw it as an extension of running comics in the paper."

Despite the media board's consternation, the three issues actually made money. "Folks who would advertise in the *CT* were folks who were very gung-ho about the Fan District and about VCU being here. They weren't looking at content. If it was getting their logo on the page, then they were happy, and this was before there were other possibilities to get published."

In addition to some of the artists who also appeared in *Graphic Showcase*, *Fan Free Funnies* included Bill Nelson, a multi-award-winning illustrator who went on to become the in-house illustrator for the *Richmond Mercury*. Other *Fan Free Funnies* artists included Trent Nicholas, Damian Bennett, Bruce Barnes, Jeff Davis, Eric Bowman, Michael Cody, Dale Milford, Stanley Garth, Joanne Fridley, Gregg Kemp, Mac McWilliams, Verlon Vrana, Ragan Reaves, Nancy Mead and Alan R. O'Neal.

Why did they stop after only three issues? "The school year ran out, or my term as executive editor ran out," said Slipek, "otherwise we would have kept going…Or maybe they shut us down, I don't remember."

Boys and Girls Grow Up, 1981–85

"I was visiting Tom Campagnoli one day, and the idea came up to self-publish a comic book," said California artist Amy Crehore. "We both collected *RAW*, a large-format graphic and comic magazine published in New York City. Tom had stacks of underground comics, and our mutual friends Anne Peet and Rodger Carrington were already publishing their own 'zines."

"I was inspired by the anthology of Arcade Comics," said Campagnoli, fully realizing the depth of comic talent in the Richmond area for a similar project. "So I thought that's really cool, we know a bunch of artists, so yea, lets do a comic book."

Boys and Girls Grow Up, number 4, 1984. Art by Amy Crehore. *Courtesy Amy Crehore.*

Eager to follow through on their idea, which they called *Boys and Girls Grow Up*, they set out contacting their artist friends for contributions for the first comics journal to appear in Richmond since the *Fan Free Funnies* had published its final issue eight years earlier. Since there was little money to publish, however, the decision was also made that if an artist wanted a comic in the magazine, they had to pony up twenty dollars to help cover printing, which was done by Richmond Printing Services on Richmond's Broad Street.

"A couple people were like, 'What? Give you twenty bucks? I'm not doing it!'" said Campagnoli. "'You should be paying me!' And it was like okay, whatever. But that was the only time we did that. From then on, we used the money from the previous issue to pay the next one."

Still, enough comic artists were found to publish a first edition in the early summer of 1981. Crehore did the black-and-white cover art, and interior comics included work by San Francisco artist Ruth Farrall and Richmond artists Mac Calhoun, Rebby Sharp, David Leslie, Anne Peet, Heather McAdams, Jude Tolley and Ted Salins. Five hundred copies were printed, and they practically sold out at $2.50 per copy.

"It was a selfish idea on my part," said Crehore. "I wanted to draw the covers and have printed samples of my art. I used the printed pieces to enter illustration competitions in New York City."

Encouraged by their success, Campagnoli and Crehore set out almost immediately producing issue number 2, which appeared in the fall of 1981. Crehore did an expensive full-color cover, and new artists inside included Leslie Carlton, Jad Fair, Jo Hoots, Trent Nicholas, Kenny Spreeman and Steve Wall, along with some of the regulars from issue number 1. The press run was upped to one thousand copies, and it sold well.

Issue number 3 appeared in March 1983. This issue, along with numbers 4 and 5, was the first of three consecutive themed issues. "We called the third one *Boys and Girls Grow Up: In the Atomic Age*," said Campagnoli, saying too that for cost control purposes they printed a spot color cover by Les Smith but still increased the print run to 1,500 copies.

After issue number 3, Crehore moved to Eugene, Oregon, making it necessary to copublish the last two issues by mail. Despite this logistic change, *Boys and Girls Grow Up #4: Dreams, Secrets and Getting Away with Murder* appeared in December 1984 with a run of one thousand copies.

The stress of publishing remotely and finances of course strained the operation. "We had our signing parties at Richmond Artists Workshop down on 1717 East Main Street, and at Plan 9 Records, we had a 'Help, We Need Money' party," Campagnoli explained.

Despite the continuing money issues, they still had one more in them, and in 1985, *Boys and Girls Grow Up #5: Illusions, Indigestion & Invisibility for All* hit the stands and the wholesalers' lists, with work by Ruth Farrall, Mary Crenshaw, V.D. Phillips, Don Bone and others. "It was number 5 that we went back to 1,500 copies," said Campagnoli, who produced this issue with Rachel Sides.

Campagnoli and Crehore unfortunately discovered, as do many small press publishers, a hard lesson from a wholesaler in Minnesota: "They said, 'Yea, we'll take like five hundred,'" said Campagnoli, "so I upped the printing, and then they said, 'Oh no, we don't need that many, we only need one hundred,' and I had already printed and paid the printer. We weren't making any money, so that kind of killed us."

There were other issues besides money at play as well. With Crehore on the West Coast making a living as an artist and with Campagnoli getting married in Virginia, it became impossible to sustain any momentum.

Unfortunately, the magazine folded just as it was gaining traction both in the mainstream press and in the underground comics world. Editor and comic artist Peter Bagge gave it a great review in *Weirdo* number 13. "There was an article in *Style* [*Weekly*]," said Campagnoli. "People seemed to really like it. And I was also selling them to a couple wholesalers, like Last Gasp in San Francisco, and they would buy fifty or one hundred." Last Gasp still lists the magazine in its catalogue, unaffected by inflation at the original 1983 list price of $2.50.

"I traveled to California after the last issue came out, and I saw them in a comic book shop in Los Angeles," said Crehore. "That gave me a thrill."

"We had discussed a twenty-five-year anniversary issue, but we missed that already," said Campagnoli. "I always wanted to do a number 6 and call it *Boys and Girls All Grown Up*."

Scratchez, 1983–86

Concerned that Richmond had not seen a real underground-style comics journal since the demise of the *Fan Free Funnies* in 1973, artist and underground comics fan Robert Lewis teamed with artist Kenny Spreeman to created *Scratchez*, a small-format comics journal that debuted in Richmond in the spring of 1983.

"I was always into making little hand-drawn storybooks and comics as a young child," Lewis said in 2013. "Later, I drifted into the science fiction and comic art fanzine realm, where I observed the efforts of amateur to semipro magazine makers, from ditto, mimeograph, to offset and later on Xerox."

Like most comic journal publishers before him, Lewis and his coproducers "tapped into the pool of artistic angst right here in Richmond" for his publication, featuring in the premiere issues familiar names like Spreeman, Alan Simons, Michael Clautice, Phil Trumbo and Rebby Sharp. A nine-year-old named Eric Stein drew an outstanding comic called *G.I.* With no set themes and wildly diverse styles, the emphasis of *Scratchez* was more to capture that underground, no-holds-barred energy of the early '70s and be taken seriously as both an artist and writer's vehicle. "It's not a straight underground comic book, it's more an idea book," Spreeman told the *Commonwealth Times*' Don Harrison in a December 1983 interview. Spreeman left the magazine after issue 3.

"Having distributed the *Washington Free Press* and *Quicksilver Times* during high school, I was familiar with the careers of the *Zap* artists and later met and became friends with many of them," said Lewis.

In a later issue, Alan Simons wrote in a quasi-editorial, "One of the reasons comics are not taken more seriously than they are…is that the publishers, editors, artists, public, etc. have failed to fully grasp that comics is a writer's medium every bit as much as an artist's medium." More artists in the later small-format editions included Helen Constance-Simon and the well-known Michael Cody, with his strip *Captain Anode*.

In the fall 1984 issue, Lewis and his new co-compiling editor Kathe Pritz switched to offset press printing and a larger eight- by twelve-inch full comic book format with a beautiful full-color process color cover by someone known only as "The Pizz." Interior strips in number 6 included a few newer Richmond-based artists in addition to the regulars, including the astonishing Hunter Jackson. Lewis's serial strip *The Making of Melba*—a sort of underground *Story of O*—appeared in almost every issue, with chapter 5 kicking off this particular issue.

After issue 8, they decided to call it quits. "We stopped for a number of reasons," said Lewis. "The overload of correspondence, shifts in territories and ownership of distributors, various economic concerns and physical exhaustion, just to name a few."

"We were burned out," Kathy Pritz said from the Richmond Antiquarian Book Shop on West Broad Street, which she and Lewis own. "Back then, it was all done by hand. I remember Bob working well into the night on a light box cutting out rubylith overlays…And besides, we were tired of eating macaroni all the time."

SOURCES

Alice. "SSOC It to Me, Baby." May 18, 1968, 4.

Associated Press. "Black Newspaper Ends Run." *Fredericksburg Free Lance-Star*, February 9, 1996, A22.

———. "Weekly Richmond Mercury Now Dead, Says Its Editor." *Fredericksburg Free Lance-Star*, September 4, 1975.

Balboni, P. Scribner. "4 'Love-Struck' Hippies Wed Here." *Richmond Times Dispatch*, October 9, 1967, State & City Section, B1.

Bass, Scott. "Ray's Light." *Style Weekly*, December 6, 2011, 1+.

Black, Michael G. "The New York Sex Papers." *Adam* 14, no. 2 (February 1970): 74–77.

Brackman, Jacob. "The Underground Press." *Playboy*, August 1967, 83+. Available at trussle.com.

Chicago Tribune. "Underground Press in U.S. Is Thriving." June 11, 1970, A10.

Cohen, Robert, and Reginald E. Zelnik. *The Free Speech Movement: Reflections on Berkeley in the 1960s*. Berkeley: University of California, 2002.

The Collegian. "Sunflower Seeds: Conley, Dorow Comment on 'Hippie' Movement." February 1968, Section 15.

Cooke, Christy. "Rash Ideas." Editorial. *Proscript*, October 18, 1968.

Creasy, Cindy. "Commonwealth Times: Good News, Bad News." *Richmond Times Dispatch*, December 7, 1980, Living Today Section, 1+.

Danky, James. "Introduction." *Undergrounds: A Union List of Alternative Periodicals in Libraries of the U.S. and Canada*. Madison: Historical Society of Wisconsin, 1974.

Editor & Publisher Yearbook. Richmond, VA: Richmond Afro-American, 1982.

Federal Bureau of Investigation. *Counterintelligence Program: Internal Security, Disruption of the New Left.* U.S. government declassified memorandums. Richmond, VA: self-published, 1968.

Fredericksburg Free Lance-Star. "Financial Troubles Close Down Mercury." August 19, 1975.

———. "Group Moves to Save Mercury." August 20, 1975.

———. "Officials Made Computer Visit." December 18, 1974.

Gitlin, Todd. *The Sixties: Years of Hope, Days of Rage.* Toronto, Ontario: Bantam, 1987.

Grimsley, Ed. "One Generation Queries Another." Editorial. *Richmond Times Dispatch,* October 2, 1967, B2.

Hayden, Tom, et al. "Port Huron Statement of the Students for a Democratic Society, 1962." Port Huron Conference of Students for a Democratic Society, Port Huron, Michigan. Michigan State University website. http://coursesa.matrix.msu.edu/~hst306/documents/huron.html.

Heale, M.J. "The Sixties as History: A Review of the Political Historiography." *American History* 33, no. 1 (2005): 133–52.

Holmberg, Mark. "*ThroTTle*'s Death Leaves Void in Underground." *Richmond Times Dispatch,* January 9, 2000, B1.

Kindman, Michael. "The Rites/Rights of Spring." *The Paper,* April 7, 1966, 1+.

Kornbluth, Jesse. "This Place of Entertainment Has No Fire Exit: The Underground Press and How It Went." *Antioch Review* 29, no. 1 (1969): 91–99.

Krassner, Paul. "An Angry Young Magazine." Editorial. *The Realist,* June 1958, 1–2.

Landes-Houff, Deona. "The Little Paper that Could." *Style Weekly,* January 10, 1989, 25.

Lewes, J. "The Underground Press in America (1964–1968): Outlining an Alternative, the Envisioning of an Underground." *Journal of Communication Inquiry* 24, no. 4 (2000): 379–400.

Lichtman, Jane. *Bring Your Own Bag: A Report on Free Universities.* Washington, D.C.: American Association for Higher Education, 1973.

Lutz, William D. *Underground Press Directory.* 4th ed. Stevens Point, WI: Counterpoint, 1970.

Mackenzie, Ross. "A Mild Form of Hippie Evening." *Richmond News-Leader,* 1968.

MacLeod, Harriet. "Not Serious." *Richmond News-Leader,* April 17, 1984, B1.

McMillian, John Campbell. *Smoking Typewriters: The Sixties Underground Press and the Rise of Alternative Media in America*. New York: Oxford University Press, 2011.

National Newspaper Publishers Association. Education Is the Best Medicine. "Hazel Trice Edney." RioVida Networks, 2008. http://www.riovida.net/channels/multi-kulti/george/EITBM-Education-8109-HazelTriceEdney2.asp.

Ozmon, Howard. "Introduction." *1973 Cobblestone Yearbook*. Richmond: Virginia Commonwealth University, 1973.

Raine, David, Jr. "Event in Park Was Wonderful." Letter to Editor. *Richmond Times Dispatch*, October 1, 1967, A14.

Rauch, J. "Activists as Interpretive Communities: Rituals of Consumption and Interaction in an Alternative Media Audience." *Media, Culture & Society* 29, no. 6 (2007): 994–1,013.

Richmond News-Leader. "Man Is Killed, 2nd Robbed in Adult Store." April 9, 1983, Area Section, 17.

———. "RPI Student Arrested." February 6, 1968.

Richmond Times Dispatch. "First Mercury Is Published." September 13, 1972, City Section, B4.

———. "Hippies Are Free to Use City Parks." October 18, 1967, Section B.

———. "Hippies Have Friend." October 10, 1967, State & City Section, B4.

———. "Judge Denies VPA's Plea to Reopen Chronicle Case." October 10, 1969.

———. "Newsboy Arrested at Beach." September 16, 1969.

———. "Vice Squad Overkill." Editorial, February 8, 1968, 13.

Ruvinsky, Maxine. "The Underground Press of the Sixties." Master's thesis, McGill University, 1995. National Library of Canada.

Shields, Todd. Associated Press. "Century Old Newspaper Advocates Black Issues." *Fredericksburg Free Lance-Star*, June 14, 1983, A8.

Spates, James L. "Counterculture and Dominant Culture Values: A Cross-National Analysis of the Underground Press and Dominant Culture Magazines." *American Sociological Review* 14, no. 5 (1976): 868–83.

Sutton, Carol. "Bang Arts Festivals." *Bang Arts Festivals*, n.d. Online at http://carolsutton.net/text/bang_arts_festivals_rpi.html.

Talley, Jean. "Agitators Unwelcome Here." Editorial. *Proscript*, November 1, 1968.

———. "Comedy of Errors." Editorial. *Proscript*, October 25, 1968.

Trumbo, Phil. "Lurking in the Hearts of Men." *Comics Journal* 103 (1985): 50+.

United States Congress, Senate Judiciary. *The Weather Underground*. 94th Cong., 1st sess. S. Rept. 0-200-898.

United States Court of Appeals, District of Columbia Circuit. *Hobson v. Wilson*, June 8, 1984. OpenJurist. http://openjurist.org/737/f2d/1/hobson-v-wilson.

Virginia Commonwealth University Board of Visitors. "Puppy Burn." *Minutes of a Special Meeting*. VCU Board of Visitors Meeting, October 31, 1968, Richmond, Virginia. James Branch Cabell Library. Special Collections and Archives, VCU Libraries.

Virginia Historical Society. "Closing Prince Edward County's Schools—The Civil Rights Movement in Virginia—Virginia Historical Society," 2004. http://www.vahistorical.org/civilrights/pec.htm.

Virginia Supreme Court. *Linwood Corbett v. Commonwealth of Virginia*. Find-A-Case, December 1, 1969. http://va.findacase.com/research/wfrmDocViewer.aspx/xq/fac.19691201_0040006.VA.htm/qx.

INDEX

ABOUT THE AUTHOR

A Shenandoah Valley native, fine arts graduate of Virginia Commonwealth University and a current graduate student in VCU's Creative Writing program, Dale Brumfield started his Richmond alternative publishing career in September 1978 as a paste-up artist, later becoming a production manager at VCU's *Commonwealth Times*. After coproducing several one-shot publications, he cofounded *ThroTTle* magazine in 1981, serving as production manager and later as editor until 1987. Dale also worked for nineteen years as a theme park technical writer and illustrator before his memoir collection, *Three Buck Naked Commodes and 18 More Tales from a Small Town*, was published in 2009. Since then, he has had two novels published: the urban fantasy *Remnants: A Novel About God, Insurance and Quality Floorcoverings* and the horror novel *Standers*, as well as two humorous e-books, *Trapped Under the Pack-Ice* and *Bad Day at the Amusement Park*. Dale has also contributed to the horror anthologies *Richmond Macabre I* and *II* and has won numerous state and national awards for his arts feature writing for the *Austin Chronicle* and Richmond's *Style Weekly* magazine, including "The Best Worst Movie You Never Saw," about his researching and finding the "lost" 1982 Richmond movie *Rock 'n' Roll Hotel*.

Dale lives in Doswell, Virginia, with his wife, Susan. His three children also attend VCU.